A PRODUCT OF INSANITY

A PRODUCT OF INSANITY

Understanding Uniform Powers,
Uniformity, Futuristic Military Dominancy
21st Century Thesis Ideological Warfare
and More……

Sylvan Lightbourne

AuthorHouse™
1663 Liberty Drive
Bloomington, IN 47403
www.authorhouse.com
Phone: 1-800-839-8640

First published by AuthorHouse 06/08/2011

ISBN: 978-1-4567-8389-1 (sc)
ISBN: 978-1-4567-8469-0 (ebk)

Printed in the United States of America

Contents

Foreword

You are about to enter a domain far vastly more than any mind has ever encountered. You the reader will soon be near to witness the greater intelligence this uniform supremists idealist has in his possession. He is also a subtractive opinion maker. This "he" is described as no other but the author of this powerful knowledge, whom, can also be called Sylvan Lightbourne.

Acknowledge reader this book is totally about me. I am considered to be a theoritician. Throughout my childhood many could not understand me and throughout time as of in today's spectrum, the few who recognizes, upon recognitioning, my intelligence do so well as to praise me. The many who has mock my intelligence entirely and neither provide a correct answer to this dilemma has remain stunned on my continuation for upgrowth, to let the world's populists regimes, learn and understand new knowledge at hand.

For my knowledge is unique and came from higher power, throughout a cosmos effect but however it may be introduced to the minds it pronounces itself as "truth" and loyalty to human intervention. It neither came from disciplines taught by minds or neither came from the hands that feed me. So unique it is, that it can be shown that as power that is confined as this, it does show potential to survive in these pressing times.

Times where all forms of prophecy before the time of the 21st century, that quintessential beings, equiped with time figuration, had to paint a picture of a more blossomed and bright colours of disasterous times ahead. Make note that what is mention here shows to you the reader ways the evolved mind can captivate any developments.

But as many of us, the uniform is one aspect but challenge upon the human aspect, no difference there can be seen. Forever during time, man combine with any uniform present: definition, ruleship, warfare, meglomaniac endeavours, creation of new warisms scriptures, called them these "war bibles" and of course not forgetting the dominion, present a warlike features in all creatures attain within the framework of living. Warlords are not created from birth, their enormous gifts and talents sometimes when not looked upon as favourite unto the unwise ones, a decptive emotion is captured and resiliency is forever unchanged.

To prove an intelligent point, the physical embodied hands with the help of the mental abilities to create, oh! What a majestic creation! To prove a point, if thousands die, well how fortunate.

For a individual to hold such a title, one must understand forehand the abilities and chaotic-cy of warfare and the effects it contributes to the make believers of unsolderists individuals. Tranversely in existence and is here to share to you the populists mind searchers that "we "do exist and to enter our minds is difficult, so do consider it a priveledge to enter this one.

So readers be eyes and ears and all other spirited energies combined to jostle and to acknowledge a new great breed of an order to come.

What you the reader must know is, this book is written to my heart's content and the language is to your fearsome desire to die in shame and disgust of yourself for denial to learn and observe, to secure and insure yourself to fall prey to captivity. Read and understand this great trait and you the reader will then make the necessary accommodations to write in your own words, how your perceptive mind thought about this endeavour.

How it is written
It shall be “read”
The way it is “read”
It should read.

Introduction

This book presented in this form can be described in many ways when put to a mind lurking to discover the truth about all types of human supremacy, however there are only three words that describes the holistic regime that is made before you the reader:

Uniformity:

-is the measure of loyalty to a system, wearing a uniform, creation of a system and the measures undertaken to keep it existing

Superiority:

-in the measure of a supreme intelligence on a battlefield, may it be foreign or domestic and superiority recognized by the skills of a people in a system

Ideology:

-in the means of logic, purely informational, the indepth searching for reasoning and the teaching of such and understanding these few attributes would open and uncover basic topics viewed by all human beings surviving in the 21st century-

It's a book to open the minds of the 21st century man, all that is 20th century and before, mostly all logic and conjectures of education are not functioning efficiently within the chaotic minds of this 21st century. So behold readers of this new domain.

Warfare:

A word which depicts to the mind seekers a fundamental issuated development brought about by emotional uncontrolled disturbance. Whereas there are all types and occupational ideology which follows war and it's attributes to survive, which is described very fortuitously and abundantly in this book.

Hence reader the book in essence contributes two parts:

Part 1—deals with every day issues, phenonenom attributes of mankind ways and their aptitude of understanding no control limitations of their innovations. All are unique knowledge described in the most literate way and to learn for the minds of man are rewarding to the reader

Part2-endowged in this profound knowledge are theories of great possibilities of uniformity and uniform governments that can exist if the right individual can harness it's energy. It will provide to the reader knowledge on how a new created system of "uniform laws" can work efficiently in the coming years of this 21st century, also it provides intellectuality, suvival training, 88th commandments and other regimic commandmental rules, war songs to cut the throats of belligerent factions, continuation of the ideology of uniform powers.

PART I

THE INFORMATIVE ART, THE ART TO TEACH

PLEDGES

A PLEDGE FROM BIRTH

I know there was a significant occurrence when I was born. The structures of the moon and the alignment of the stars hence forth allows their bright appearance to shine upon me, gifts far escalated towards any mind searchers within this domained world. I from birth had only to exercise its power during my exercising of my mind to childhood days-adult life-retiring days. But from birth, this significant one, this superior child, blessed in awe and wonder. It's only to this, I, to combat his earthly human traits of emotions to get what's richly his. The opportunity to change what is in existence to a perfect existing existent.

A PLEDGE TO CHILDHOOD EXPERIENCE

I singularly, an outstanding child who fit perfectly amongst those who subsequently unfit well in an area filled with books and teachers to read it unto us. This eyeing child, this beautiful child hits childhood experience without a hope to meet friends or have any to play, to chat, to experience what it is to feel special. Born without the help of a helping hand carried upon without a hand to help. This childhood experience without friends to chatter upon, outcasts from small it had begun. So we shall see for this teenagers feats.

A PLEDGE TO TEENAGER EXPERIENCE

A "rebel" disguised in uniform, school uniform assembling in classrooms filled with multi ethnic I's similar in age, un similarity in what I posses within my mind. A rebel when spoken to, rebellious to all form and fashion to school adoptancy of rules and regulations. Create his own, the dominance that scored the scholars the controlled mind of these professors and their shirt collars. Join a group-hardly—I taught my domain to be a singular soldier. A soldier "I" a one army I who defeat all group I's. A figure to be looked upon hardly wished upon by elders who see elsewhere but attempts to look through inside here, the blackened heart. His gifts tarnished until some day he sees his potential to become super superior I.

A PLEDGE OF ADULT HOOD

A day of many challenges to look for a work, a paying work to achieve a paper currency that holds many hands. A currency that sees every life, been into every home, into every pocket and sees how the ones who achieve it spends its value of worth. Hence posses the gift to see behind the mask, which is the mind.

The mind behind the mask, faces challenges everyday, the mind which lay dormant within every human being who allows it to think endlessly for their decision here within the system to make money, gravitational currency. A special day of changing work, changing the amount "I" work for. The spending "I" has a lot on his mind to save for betterment or spend on entertaining "I" a lavish life style. For I have forgotten all my possessive gifts.

A tomorrow day come, wisdom come, it hit my head, the last day I wrote some notes was during my experience in my teenager years "those rebellious years". That for some reason brought out a laying foundation out of me, an art to learn about creating ideas and ideals, my gifts indeed had hit me once, where I have forgotten, hit me twice, for which I have remembered. Had so I continued my destination of becoming a super superior "I".

A PLEDGE OF THE CHALLENGING DAYS AHEAD

Super superior "I" woke up one day and realized "I" have written two books. My first book which posses errors and continuation of it occurs but to the mind that reads it, how few it is have understand great altitude which suddenly impeded in their lifestyle of living.

A life style where the world events exist and a collection of superiorness infamy exists. So as such one must be at their peak of understanding powers that exist within one "I" where individual I's are becoming empires of their own.

Equipped with machine of mans tyranny. Hence my second book deals with the power of an existing uniform warlord, where these warlord traits are considered powerful enough to be recognized as the one to create Armageddon. This book a very omnipotent script has devised "I" as a tyrant in my own way, prophesying warlike behaviour amongst a stable enterprise.

Blasting my views and hypocriting my endeavours as creating a new religion, therefore "I" a superior "I" take not their critical critic lines at boring hearts. For what "I" spell out is no different to what the ages have seen. So destroying "I" yet to see.

I pledge allegiance to only "I", for before and continue to my desired pledges are to better my skills with the stronghold battles who lie silently till that day of damnation seeks its face amongst mankind.

WARRING "I"

PERSONAL NOTES

Personal notes on the idea of "I" a human being—

Born out of the womb of a woman called her "mother" to make "I" the collaborated effort made during sexual excitement caused the hormone gland to produce its contents, therefore laid within a womb of a growing sustenance, the effort made by a man called him my "father".

I so weak am I that it must be made that two human beings made time to create "I". For they do not know yet or maybe they do, that "I" must attain the leadership of a supreme human being in thoughts and ideas in evoluted motions and the skills to the continuated survival to what "I" posses.

To "I" do not consider myself to be just human but super human. Maybe the idea came out to be sometimes, that "I" am a species of God like features, to "I" think the abnormal but why do "I" consists of all human attributes to live, to eat, to breathe, to grow but my intelligence consists of a different growth itself.

Separated from the likes and functions of the operation of my body. But these thoughts have rekindled my effort more to acknowledge that flesh and bone "I" am but legacy to attain and remain would prove that "I" was here. More attainment produces more enjoyment of understanding life, life's goals, achievements, which brings productivity at all levels. So this brain that "I" posses but fail to use such then "I" ask them, let me feed on yours?

If you don't need it. Super superior "I" was born, super superior "I" still am and a legend I am hoping to be.

"Can there be a thoughted idea where "I" a human being can fuelled a synopsis to grow from a weak species to that of a superior one?" do "I" have to undergo scientific experiments to become more than human or do "I" have to take it to another level to ensure am ready for any battle from any individual claiming that their embodied "I" is ready for a challenge.

To claim a challenge one must know their favourite skill, that is left behind until the battlefield becomes equal in strategies, for "I" do not have to profess this knowledge. These individual "I's" there are all over, always trying to manipulate a growing strategy at work, always seeking small conversations, attempting to find out your greatest strength. Neither do "I" find time to either discuss my plans. My plans are not for you at first hand, you individual "I's" would see it in the battlefield.

These individual I's challenging this super superior "I", what a laugh this shall be, for "I" yes "I" consider myself to be more, yes more, yet to achieve more, this motivation must be stored in the brain, so the brain would have no other choice to find ways to adhere to the individuals calling to search to become a legend.

Personal notes on the idea of "I" an omnipotent enterprise—

An enterprise can be considered as a network of different authorities and their many functions but to apply the word enterprise to describe the many supreme actions of an individual can be a development to create a lot of disliked atmosphere, created only by your individual I's surrounding you. Well who said competitions was not a great feat to encounter and wish upon? The omnipotent "I" do not wish upon the stars for competitors to arrive, "I" the supreme "I" only have to say such words only to derogate their humanity of being less intelligent, similar to those on four legs.

Anti I's all over and their works are always anti, so are their use of their brain, every aspect they decide on are always oppositional. The opposition can never be opposed, for such are their possession to oppose all that is created by these superior I's.

For a human enterprise consists of a self discipline look on traits of hidden skills adapted for only last resort kill. Yet the enterprise which can be made within these individual minds housed these enterprise but they have to create many doors towards the source to ensure that limitations are met to these anti I's, if overgrownment are met.

Human enterprise, for not many posses such traits, yet few wants such traits but to do what? A practice few are taught and many who searches for its answers. The omnipotent enterprise which catastrophically are hidden in I's who are born by birth encrypted with abilities of all powerfulness. So if one superior I can tell you an individual I about an enterprise he is in possession off, bet your life is about to get ugly!

Personal notes on the idea of "I" a fueling war between two powers of good and bad—

I who rubs shoulder to shoulder, I who shakes hand well with others who love to; debate on all conformities of the inventitive continuation of mans existence. I who shelters my body from the rain drops of cries of many I's in the domain of life's troubles

To much to hear to the greater I's that stomps on the lesser I's, so must the lesser I's feed of the crumbs of the greater I's. Their good intelligence which lacks fortune but rewards are fortitutional.

The world full with powerful I's, individual mongols trapped in their disillusioned ideas. Some powerful I's get strapped on with some power, so go to the field and explode these powers in a mass of people who posses little knowledge of the works of mankind.

These good I's, these are the ones who profess a different temperament to the journey of life. These wicked I's who only seek vengeance to others who seek not their ways, self absorbed to their ways, their wavery ways. Their products are seen; make mass hysteria around the world.

Then there are these laughing I's, these joyous I's, make no mistake they posses no knowledge but use their energy only to exercise their mouths to smoke every degree of products to battle their image, their weak image. Take life for a joke to all system contains many of them just waiting to be destroyed by super superior "I".

A fueling war between good I's and bad, a funding fueling war made possible by both individual I's to ensure a balance between the energies of the world. An endless tiresome war made between the voids that distorts the idealist that survival are made when I's of this individual space we occupy must participate in occurrence of this between war, where all individuals are left in the middle to choose which power "I" shall chose to super instill my cause of being a superior "I".

Personal notes on the idea of "I" the creator of a new regime—

Let's roll the dice and take our chances, let's prepare for battles knowing we can never win the war but hoping we can, create, endeavours far greater than you the individual I's can ever imagine. A newly regimic to be born, one where intellectual values portrays a pinnacle structure to such a regime, where the individual who holds the mantra of the regime can be counted as supreme I's who knows about battlefields and a winning strife to attain free leadership to war.

An "I" in war, an individual that loves war is order to institute a new regime one must be out of the picture. Isn't war an option to institute new authority? Well if so, the I's shall go brave and do well to attain free leadership to war.

A regimic I, an, I who only involve himself in new creation on this self made system of mankind, making him a legendary I. To become legendary, the I must fist pick a system which must be destroyed or further be annihilated from the free thinking of the idealist I's.

A regime where I "the supreme being I", sees that since the creation of inventions, one can clearly see a trait of destruction where "I" must not say, for I shall hence the reward and axed the heads who dare the only I who posses the willing winning solution to see it's growing abilities above the rest of these other regimic I's. These I's must be erased, the new creators of I's who will resemble the super superior "I".

Personal notes on the idea of "I" in war and war in "I"—

As "I" an individual soldier who represent truth, justice, honor, survival, a battlefield can never be justified as an end to a means, and to a dying cause, where all playing I, forms their formation and engage in trickery warfare to it's highest repertoire.

So as "I" a walk in this direction shall enlighten I more to understand that life is a battle in its own way. To discover its meaning I's and the other I's involve in this warring of I's must sight all pronunciation and engage fully to this cause.

This 21st century where all I's want to be a combattorial, serving a cause of any corrupt dilemmas, so as such, I's shall never rethink that forming your own personal warring improves your generation of offspring's ability to understand survival.

The gift of improvisation, where war is not a faction, any I, who seeks improvement must be bewildered about when first sighting occurs. So as such one must be glorious, one can participate in this glorifying "warring I" where there can never be a good or bad individual I, in a battlefield. All I's wearing amour fit for battle represents the same force of opponents, don't make the judgement wrong, some are good or bad, their can be no causes in a battlefield. You the individual "I" are there to show the other opponent I's who better the skills in training and who represents the shield of honor more bravery, to be counted one of the best, individual I, to be renamed or named as a legend, in history of time and giving names to those who deserve it.

Personal notes on the idea of "I" a great emissary to the wanna be great I's—

When you the wanna be great I's on notice see great powerful I in front view, then bow down entirely you shall or else I will declare battorial warfare on you the wanna be great I's.

Salvation of prayers will not be at your side, providing “amour” to your involved war that you, the wanna be great I have created without prior knowledge that the world that surrounds us, the soldier of I, with such immense power, they will always exist a time where all individual I’s shall meet a battle of intelligence and skills personalized with your own knowledge on experience of warring I’s.

You warring I’s with no pronounced knowledge of your inner skills, your great weakness of not being too experienced with battling warring I’s like I. Wanna be great I’s—for greatness are not meet for everyone—seeing these I’s using all optimum of cherished skills to make adaptations to be a superior I—make doubtful attempting of doubting I—a supreme superior I that was fueled by rage and born with a gift of combativeness and a strength un norm to these individual I’s.

The coming of this I would be no more of a welcome by the signs that are shown, “I” is already here.

Personal notes on the idea of “I” an everlasting eternal fire within—

I posses maximum total of spark within my body to engage my inner I to handle any immerse emissary “I”, watch them come a thousand mile, one I called upon, many I to engage in battlery warfare amongst I and I alone.

For I cannot think little of this situation, this burning spark within I allows “I” to have superpower to destroy a thousand I’s who only objective is to put upon a trophy wall. The eternal fire which dwells within any favourite combatant I’s, familiar with the works of battlery. Singularly if a thousand I under the influential domain hopes to achieve a winning situation to destroy “one” I, then objectively this I must be a very powerful, so as such one "I" cannot destroy him, a thousand can, hopes to think it can be possible. The eternal fire resounding within this warring I.

Personal note on the idea of "I" a king conqueror all—

King of battle and aims for battles, thrust fear within conquers and face with conquerors and pace on battlefields and race to see if opponents are erase. I a king conqueror battles those who pronounce themselves conqueror of honour and truth to these inner desires founded astounders. The battle within I a conqueror king, this warrior within the I infinite, to conquer all. A lot of war suppresses the mind to solitude and destitute pronounced inferior but ulterior beliefs.

CHAPTER I

WAR

WARS TRUE MEANING {part 1}

War is a deadly price to pay, since it stimulates the mind into shock or of fright behavioural power, which inhibit the enemy or the combatant to forget the sense of morality in so being in a loss unamoured field which he may not aim to defeat but be susceptible for a defeat, by a less contemptible force of natures way that death comes to everyone

Those who are weak get putted down

Those who are strong, gets to live another day.

For that is the way of a soldiers living, a way that camouflage is an item of a choice decision or favourable, to be admired and respected of character, be liked by your worst enemy for not be able to strike at the heart but a mind setting attitude brings any enemy down.

You choose if he should live or die but by death pays a deadly price and war should be carefully looked at before attempted by man. War is a character of its own and power feeds on war greedily puts you on knees in shame and disgust of yourself causing pain and suicidal acts. To any defiant of legit command, learn about world wars and study it, because any day could be a war. Advisable by anyone, learn how to survive and handle yourself in care amongst any one who intent to continuously hurt the body.

The mind is a powerful gift, don't waste its ability to survive. The universe can give and take you away, let them remember you for what you've done. A war is far understandable by you but perfectly underminded by me a "soldier".

{1} The introductory of caliber weaponry is either taught or of learned circumstances, on fault defaults voices which are abrupt patterns which triggers the on property to a fistful offence, priority, to win a unnoticed battle, child play or adult play, ages don't matter where mechanical machines takes over the fistful hands, on reached, to defend the outer body, and the "in" attached to the body likewise the disruptor of any kind disturbs the trajectory patterns of the soft tissue of the body. The veins, the arteries where I have undertook lessons that should say the great god have not made the body to fight or kill but a body too use wisely under god. Think the use to be brave makes mechanical machines to be used in battle.

{2}learn what's taught and not use what's taught to harm or injure but to disarm and physically put at rest for the movement of discharge. The bigger the status overhead, hangs a bigger responsibility, the use of the body over circumstances likewise the larger body but less use of the brain is "performance showed" by some leaders when situation occurs, overhead thinking goes 100% ahead than their body, when the use of physically violence is showed.

{3} dialect atrocities proven to be a worse sidekick, through develop formalities against newly improved laws of humanities. Look upon every house developer of man and disguise no anger towards a soldier building their own, of small proportionalities or of huge egos. If of a young impressionative mind shows huge thinking no matter being disliked or out of order, he can be an important being in the future because what is taught is learned systematically and use it to combat any formula but if you go outside the box, and improve your learning you can indeed learn unsystematically. One point in war is at all disused and properly misused, for war is not battle but battle for power causes immense war. Many have you seen leaders coming forward that are respected by even the educators because of charged situations. Underground is used to learn from mistakes and a home is used to plan for a future.

THE UNDERUNDERGROUND {part2}

The underground takes many form-{1}educate{2}hide—to change drastically forms of body structure.

[1} educate-education on knowledge to remain subtle and learn new materials on any particular raw subject may take substantially any amount of years not days or weeks, minimal amount are two to five years of recovery and rewinded learning. Learning underground brings pride, lots of effort and work but demanding power for knowledge brings any so called persons down when having to undertake tremendous pressure of your learning abilities. Learning must be strenuous and must take any form of documentaries-letters-music-information on reliable communicable sources.

{2} hide-many persons hide or create new identities living underground. Many use hiding to defend themselves against possible attacks to bring any battlers down. Brings relief and sudden panic attacks when hiding may not feel that your not learning alot as it brings pressure and uncomfortness and means to attack first comes to be a great risk, when years of hiding for means that are unknowned, causes permanent effects that are lifetime phenomenal of anger.

AFFIRMATION

As a soldier coming up in the world, you must not get to excited with the ideas put forth by certain governmental institutions called systems with a name to govern people. You must challenge yourself to be better, more outstanding let "MILITARY ENFORCEMENT RULE". You must show confidence to be an idealist and bring out new ideas to improve "soldierrism" in the world.

SOLDIERRISM-is the study of preferences of warfare both doctrinally and battlery, to which their only honour goes to a existing system or government.

WARS TRUE CULTURE WHICH BRINGS FORTH MEANING

CULTURE-culture for "pain", culture for "war", culture to "die", years of intact schematics, knowledge to condemn any opponents ideas that supportive construed master plans for destruction, is always to whom can show supreme adoption of life's regime. Observance of soldiers being involved in civil past wars against their own governments and seem to be right in their ways. Are governments likewise all over the world of uncontrolled opinions are the causes of their own inner problems-the coup-e-tat,-the over thrownments,-the genocide, the killings for prolonged years. Governments are not a system with balance insertive methods to re-position themselves after any deterrent adoption by their own citizens.

NOTE TO WORLD: The world is small but unique, the world have been through a lot from man developing ideas and worshiping these ideas, even profiting from these ideas, to use to destroy their counterparts. The world have seen man inherit inventions from automobile to bridges to cities to airplanes to spacecrafts to satellites, to the creation of ruleship, but can the world hold against the tiresome efforts put forth by man, place yourself at any location in the world and witness if you are safe from tyrannies.

NOTE TO WORLD: This generation that seeks growing was the yesterday, new development of a new chapter once seen in your eyes and your children eyes. A new century has been born, one that inherits new tactical spirited enforcers that life means nothing, neither the scriptures on life can without their destruction for their made bodies. Not a prohibitation, not to have families but varieties of comfort and desires that elimination of a single goal is not interfered or rebuked by their abrupt actions for love.

Government rulers forgets the policies of true leadership and provokes any incumbent, foolish leader and adheres to war. In the beginning, signs are shown-bewilderment are shown-curiosity are bestowed. Creating incorporated alliance outside the law would grow-indeed, so powerful that generations to come, show signs of terrorists would take place. No longer would judiciary empower but single acts passed in governments would caster retribution.

Many occasions these atrocities occurs leaving debates impossible and irreplaceable. The patriots are left stranded and to defend themselves by all possible means, whereas over the years independent separatists group are formed-no longer seeking protection from the government.

Inventionists would be found proclaiming that knowledge would take control of man's old thinking of not introducing new knowledge over the era's of yesterdays and today.

AFFIRMATION

A PARADISE IS WHEN ALL FORMS OF IDEAS ARE FORGIVEN,FOR WAR ARE A SUCCULENT PERFORMANCE OF ONE'S DESIRES,DESTROYING THAT DESIRE YOU WOULD OF CONQUER THE ONLY THING STANDING BETWEEN THOUSANDS OF DEATH AND BILLIONS.

AN IDEAL OF OATH TO SELF-

{1} I will believe in the one belief that now in my life, that I can fully taste my willingness—strongest at my heart, to not ask for any desired help from no enemies-apartied friends or other embodied individuals in the world.

{2}I will strongly believe in my beliefs to use the only service of knowledge to combat any on willing opponent-and defeating these soldiers would be a fun action and a must.

{3} I will withhold the ideals of my gift and inherit it to the furthest extent as a main contributor of help to the rightless world.

AFFIRMATION

A world order, when all dominations are shown and the characters are lewd to adornment, risen favouritetism—practicism would be acknowledge to their only dyer need to survive standing in front of bravery, to defend the nations citizens behind in patriotism, in their more less contemptible theory. The advocation at its greatest.

POWER

THE POWER OF THE MIND BEYOND COMPRESSION

You can call it gifts or curse, but instinct feelings of becoming leaders, not withstanding that you are still recognised as a person. But, we, are given opportunies to abridge ourselves {the cursed} ones to evolve into a good or of a sinister aggressive lifestyle. Our power is great, yet not forgetting the efforting time for our accomplishment. Banishment would be seen, for they do not understand that we would inherit our mindful tactics onto the world. Perilous disasters, the havoc world, would be crumbled into dust and washed away by the blood of quiet provocation, which is at its fullest. And let it be that whosoever that are not chosen, would sacrifice all means necessary to convert it into a new consumption by dissolving it onto the new generations-familiar, likewise as your children.

NOTE: The genre of the world and its survival over the years is its adoption of the mind and the performance of the beholders intelligence to keep it revolving.

BASIC LITERACY-on EGOTISM-of CONQUERING ENEMIES DORMAIN{B.L.E.E.D}

The level of intelligence would be mines for the taking. Commandments-regulations-a berserk dominator for inflicting speculative speech to infidelic minds—{the mind comes a doorway—some are open to receive entry, some are locked with the very untouched memories of life} where is the direction, the guidelines of entrapments. When's not in usage-give optimum chances of overstepping into battlefield zone, filled with fires of wild ideas—when touched, gives off enormous sparks of horrors. Each one have a story to tell. An advisable comment to listen, what reasonable doubts in possession, in adoption, are fundamental issue of sub-command mental rule of thoughts of war, the performationknown as the art-to design, the ability to craft seemingless thoughts to destroy rules, reveling status to untouched statue of legit appraisal.

AS THERE CAN BE NO TWO EQUAL HEADS OF POWER IN ONE ROOM NOR THERE CAN be NO ONE HEART TO DESTROY.

THE POWER OF DETERMINATION: This particular power is "THE MOST ELUSIVE" power of all. The power for succeeding the thoughts, the ideas, to bring it to ideas of reality and misbeliefs. Condemnation likewise, confirmation up wise, throughout named history, powerful acts done by hideous individuals, were first planned, schematically through the ideal planning, that provide thousands of reasoning but anticipation and longing hate, reputed this act to reality. The 21 St century, the period of ideas and the usage of the intelligent mind that makes room for expansion too achieve earthly desires.

THE POWER TO BE GREAT: Is to make something of nothing into gold's of valuable illusions, with the idea to achieve greatness, from inner beliefs and inner strengths to absolve a mechanical grasps that the disillusioned civilians are just reflections of generations of failure to improve their standard of great. Yesterday-aim to be great

Tomorrow-is to achieve great

Future-is holding the power of great, in the eyes of your reflections given of by the mirrors of failure to come, expect the unexpected—for this is just how the world revolves.

THE POWER OF SUPREME INTELLIGENCE: Extent the mind into possibilities, abridge from the normally of learning. The governmental learning is but of small and unique in it's failure to compromise its efforting wastage among individuals, that seems to not have any motivations of learning. Supreme intelligence comes from keeping individuals that plagues the world with evilous crime "to where does supreme intelligence comes from?" it comes from separation of the mind and refilling this capability with reasoning and contradictory statements by means of words like 'hate, lusts, boldness'. At a young age so development of intelligence would grow sufficiently, when attending further studies, against the institutionalized curriculum career of your own governments. Separatists ideas are very founded to improve status of supreme intelligence. Extravagant behavior is an opted gift when years of preparations and knowing, what pertains the power to govern oneself, making possible combat schemes against the combatant, who wishes to defy your already existing power, Challenges must be at a high, in order to test your intelligence maximally.

THE ART OF LIVING IS AN CAMOUFLAGE WITH THE USE OF IT, ITS AN ART OF SILENCE

The power of subtly, is the utmost, foremost, power which is born to defeat any individual that wishes to contest it's willing existence.

NOTE:

FORCES OF POWER WOULD GREET US WITH HANDS OF FLAMES, MIND OF DARKNESS FEETS OF SPEED, TONGUE OFPREPAREDNESS AND THE IDEA OF "DEATH" releases symptoms of sickness to human weakness, for the gifted one The power of curse would guide them to total REVOULUTION and causes of REVOLVILUTION.

CHAPTER II

PRINCIPALITIES

ANTHEMS-Are a form of stylish writing, which brings to the reader a beauty of feeling for regulative distribution-due to its effect of its commanding style writing.

Regimental beholders, neither agree that their privileges are overlooked, primarily to produce, secondary fits, the likes of the people, living under common rule is common, outcasters, internationals sky seekers for productivity towards nationless thinkers. Barricading historical knowledge on progressiveaggression seemingly looked as an attempt to become differentiated in political views.

NOTE: Pinnacle-animosity-to characters-un forgiveness while corrupted, yet beauty comes from portrayal of a smile, their deadly words-ampled as survival tactics, that opponents rages supremely—unjustly and orthodoxly. Prevention is apted and tempted to plot plays of devestation to many and not one. For one is a small test, that should not be desirable componently, elementaly with fascination factors. To calmness brings light intelligent information, which perhaps shows no present form of annihilation—for presence of hatred, malice, thoughts and ideas of damnation. CLASSIFICATION OF AN ENEMY-or COMBATOR Firstly an enemy is someone whose been given life, gifts, the will power to exceed the limitation of living succeedingly profitable. It can be classified as any person here on earth. It comes sayingly noted in religious scriptures, that an enemy is not an ally of "your" interest of growth. Someone who vehemently, propose destruction to your life, without any prior knowledge of existence. To "enemy" is a strong word used rapidly and untamed.

NOTE: If one is to be combated, then the describe word to be used onto the combated/the defeated is a "enemy" in a retrospective view. Subsidingly no other person is involved or no equal powers of strength are involved.

CASTING HANDS IN SIMPLE TEST OF BOILING WATER-PITCHES THE HANDS FEARFULLY AND QUICKLY RUN TO COOL ITS HURTFUL EFFECT

Depths of eliminated controlment: There is no limations towards the effects the hands can take in the steam water and if warriorism evolves outcastment of the hands seems not possible, it will hurt. So it is with the brain, there is a control pressure the brain can absorb and the decision is yours, if you can take the control pressure over the limits of hurtful pain. For the brain is not like the senses that removes when in danger, to test your knowledge, test your brain, you must never uptake to coolment.

Pit of agonative condemnation: The pit terminology means the declaration for war, bestowed by the comb ator, to ensure if the defeated can reassemble the destructive mind and fight for the nation at bay "patriotically". It is the very last means of the "analystic theory", while the simple hate people portrays becomes noticed by power beings, and seeing this, it evolves more powerfully, their resemblances are of their own but a revolutionary, mutates all power, which becomes a personality and causes lives to be lost. For times that are ahead incinerates the flowdarity of good and when comes simple tasking, devours temptations of reputable followers.

OPPORTUNITIES AND WHEN THEY ARRIVES

Opportunists activities are bestowed when tools of bewilderment are shown as a character and "sleep" are endowged. The "hunters" make presence their face to be known and captivity to the "hunted". For this is the way of the thickened blood that sustains the will of a soldier in combat. Government training or self-taught, are both SHIELDS OF BATTLERY that are overlooked by the "citizenry" of closed battorial nations BATTORIAL NATIONS: Hostility-the drama of plays and harmonic deaths. Barbarism-the vicious acts to slay many uncountered combators, to put their bloods to a direly shame. They are nations that seek the use of both hostility and barbarisms as a golden outcome of diplomacy. Tied with the viciousness outbreak of initializing two heads against each other to a dated argumentum thrills of cunningness, wittiness, their intelligence going beyond the displacement of a approach of governments interference. These heads on struggle for uniqueness of "symbolism" of greater domination domain of punishing on the upper hand of true "flager patriotism" or flagerism.

FOR THE "WAR" MAKES ME FEEL TO BE "INEVITABLE"
MAKES ME SEE TO BE "INCREDIBLE"
MAKES ME TASTE THE "INTOLERABLE"
MAKES ME DESTROY THE "INFIDELABLE"
MAKES ME PLAY THE "INSTRUMENTABLE"
BATTTORIAL NATIONS {command orders}

{1}To defend at will.

{2}To inhibit a sense of openness to "death"

{3} To witness the feeling of death

{4}To not die in shame and disgust

BATTORIAL PUNISHMENTS: The reigning moments when all are defeated from the corners of the south to the north-to the east and to the west. Comes only songs of defeat and slaughters. In only their last desperations-talks began on how to retake what's been conquered. Alliances are formed but stands out as minimum damage they can only offer.

SECTORIALISM: It is noted that governments comes at all forms, not forgetting the "system" governing these portfolios of true "governance". Sectorialisation comes powerful, especially when it's identity is unknown.

MILITARY AFFIRMATION on OCCUPANTS Desires of CHAOTIC-cy {M A 0 C}

The warmongers-the peace makers-the people that hide their true motives of successes. The world would always be corrupted, while the systems regenerates itself by anxious industrious minds, capable of exercising the rights to be fearless when tasks are been putted forth.

GOLDEN RULE: {1}

OUR SUCCESSES ARE BUT OUR OWN AND NO ONE'S ELSE'S OWN-TO BELIEVE-OTHER WOULD

BE A DAMNATION TO-SELF-THE DESTRUCTION OF THEIR OWN.

GOLDEN RULE :{2}

MY SUCESSES ARE BUT MINES AND NO ONE'S ELSE'S OWN-TO BELIEVE-OTHER-WOULD BE A DEFIRMATION TO SELF-THE DESTRUCTION OF THEIR OWN SHADOW-HIDING BEHIND MY SUCCESSES.

GOLDEN RULE {3}

MY SUCCESSES ARE MINES AND MINES ALONE-THE SYSTEM OF MAN'S DESTRUCTION-THE CREATION OF MY SUCCESSES WOULD BE AN EVERLASTING ONE.

GOLDEN RULE: {4}

FOR IF MY FEARS ARE WORSE—THEN LET IT BE TOWARDS—INEXPERIENCE-AND NOT EMOTIONS-CAPTURED BY FAILURES OF RIVALRIES

THE—I's—in the EYES

The I's are the "is note" an individual must do to not make the same mistakes twice. For i the individual accepts no defeat, which would come along the way of your victories.

{a}The I's—is the "formula" for i-success-or your success {b} The I is the symbol, showing "correctiveness" of positioning—on the spot, and being decisive on you work

{c} The I is winning superiority, that remains unchanged NOTE TO WORLD: To remember during the evolution on man battlery has always stood its way against all attempts of the usage of certain persons goal for "empires". Now even, before, intelligence and forms of battlery has join together to form "military"-to that of military, are to secure the parliamentarians goal of governance and it "supporters". Always remember battlery is a system grown on its own. For many years the human dominance fail to see that controlling "battlery forces" for their own purpose, brings forth new plagues of existing thought-where expansion of the mind, creates objects and seeks governance of battlery forces to contain their pleasures of security. Now military looks upon like a new embodied system, feeding off their governments, and uses the participants in "death missions", not favourable to that of their own. To fight in "honor" and not die "despicably" in the hands of combators, whose history of violent acts, rapes cities and survived decades upon decades through, through walls of terror. Singular men of hate, now seeks military for their own dominated usage, to that of security of their nations and non-participants who are regarded as civilians-whose lives are never considered as "case of emergency".

The effects of wars, especially world wars are that systems are mutated. The usage of weapons by citizens for wrong attributes, and for men who creates them de with their successes. Not even knowing how to defeat or challenge their successors, who posses enormous strength and intelligence of battlery

SING SONGS FOR THE LIVING & SING SONGS FOR THE DEAD FOR YOU MUST NEVER FOLLOW IDEAS BUT LET IDEAS FOLLOW YOU

CHAPTER III

INTRODUCTION OF THE INVENTITIVE MINDS

NOTE: To be an inventor, to feel emotionally scarred, to the activities done to the inventor's work, the achievement done to seduce the inventors intelligent mind of up growth Non the less, the perpetrators of the intolerable, injustice on the inventors invention without knowledge of the determine dedication to "create"-or day of remembrance is appalling. To this I believe, to no abominator of any kind of unknown intelligence, would use my intelligence without knowing the struggles, I have faced with tremendous, blackened mind, would be given the fall of first witnessing its power. To that power wielded by another power would triumphantly create an enormous catastrophic element, to that element are the stepping stone to apiliate sources captured by mans stability, man sustainity, man of hate, man of division, men that divide.

LET THE INHABITANTS OF THIS WORLD SEE-THE WORLD IS FOR "SURVIVALISTS" IF YOU CAN'T SURVIVE-I SUGGEST YOU GO HIDE LET THE INTERVENTIONS OF INVENTIONS REIGN-FOR LET THE COMPLENTARY DISGUSTS OF HUMAN EMOTIONS, SHY AWAY GOVERNMENT AND GOVERNANCE

Government-Is the system used, whereby ruleship of order of embodied bodies, dictates all concepts of philosophical wisdom and adopts the "human conduct" approach, too which all collectively are one strength of "force". A system of great power, "mans, most greatest invention" which is not insurmountable to any degree of human intelligence, but looked upon for sustenance exceeding the amountable, so as performation would be accounted for. The highest form of "mans system of inventions, on the intervention" of ruleship of no other but the inhabitants of the generations now to the generations then.

Governance-Survives only when the existence of their type of government is still evoluting. To continue this evolution, comes only by the persons in power or the heads of state are chosen to lead the term of office into successful years. But due to man's errors over the years of the worlds existence, governments are classified differently only by their "types" and their "failures" of types of governing in the history of interventions. And to this, these types of governments are given bad reputational names of their ruleship performance and lack of discernment and therefore intelligence, that contributed in diverted passionate patterns that do not consists in modern patterns of surviving in this 21 St century. INVENTIONS-Capabilities use for survival and for betterment of mankind.

CREATIONS-To create, to accommodate

INVENTORS-Intelligent beings who posses the attributes to invent.

CREATORS-Human beings who create/make-within reflection of what is present.

LAWS OF MAN: To law was invented by the philosophical educators of the past, whom has seen victory of conquest available within the system, whereby kings and queens, rulers of their people and their explorations world wide, but to coincidence the kingship rule periods were in danger so introducing "independency" and their republic rulement, so introducing governance and governments. To these philosophical separated the powers of the king and place them at their own domains, for controlment of human beings, who are themselves human being, who better to understand. Separation are

{1} Acted in parliament

{2} Constituted in the judicial

{3}Instituted by the policing

Citizens themselves creates their own laws in reprisal of the laws within the government, so adhering survival is at a maximum level to these citizens, so contributing in acts in defense of the oppressional laws governing their statue of living. To these laws created by citizens, so affects the young citizens of the nation, so adhering to young offenders with a impressionate mind that the people in governance creates a system of to much controlment, they don't feel emotionally freedom for living. To these feelings are the emotional disturbance captivated by these citizens.

NOTE: For what man should never do is, to apologize for occurrences for horrific actions done unto "man in the past"-for man today, you where not present in the past-for man now, you are here present. For the past occurrences is to what creates the future, which are the man of today. For the ways of man yesterdays could off never been better for what it was, to even participation of good minds or that of evil.

THE MAN OF TODAY: The man of today always finds solice, pride, greed, temptation to what man needs. The inventors of the past where not in hindrance when it comes to betterment of human lives, for they are the ones who "now" have the world in sustainity. For the inhabitants of the world "today" take the easy life for granted, for they themselves make contribution to the world but they inflict selfish loathe to the system in existence, thinking they have accomplished a lot.

WHEN TOO MUCH HANDS COMES TOGETHER TO CREATE THE "INEVITABLE"—IT CORRUPTS THE "CREATED"-THEN IT SPOILS THE "CREATION"

To man of today cannot control the ideas of man of yesterdays, unless the man of today sees their usefulness of the ideas and concoct these ideas to form an illusionistic, rejuvenation of what was always there-how possible to create an invention of something which was not a formation of balance within the world of today forgotten by man of yesterdays.

A COMMAND PLEDGE: SIMPLE ARE MEN—MAN OF DUST, SIMPLE ARE MEN-MAN AND THEIR THOUGHTS, SIMPLE ARE MEN—MAN AND THEIR SUPERIORITY, SIMPLE ARE MEN-SIMPLE THEY ARE—THROW WORDS AT GOD, SO SIMPLE THEY ARE-THROW WORDS AT MAN, SUPERIOR THEY ARE SIMPLE ARE MEN-MANS WORDS OF THEIR LIFE, MAN WORDS OF THEIR GOD, MAN WORDS, THEY SAY-THEY OBEY GOD MANS WORDS-THEY SAY, THEY—LIVE FOR-THIER GOD SIMPLE ARE MEN, GODS WORDS PUT MANS LIFE TO AN END—SO SIMPLE ARE MEN-

CHAPTER IV

REVELATIONS

MYSTERYS OF KNOWLEDGES

There are profound ways a being can introduce knowledge unto such a beings already intelligent brain to these controlled means are

{1}CREATED KNOWLEDGE: Knowledge created by some ingenious being of the past thus introduced by the minds of the future-for some means it may be of great importance to the minds of the future.

{2} INGROWN KNOWLEDGE: Knowledge that a being impose unto another, resulting in controlled behavior.

{3}LEARNT KNOWLEDGE: Knowledge that are in result of the human dilemma of the use of a very important medium called "conversations".

{4}DISCOVERED KNOWLEDGE: Knowledge that are found by an intelligent being during an expedition or mistakenly found by such a being.

{5}COMMON INSTINCT KNOWLEDGE: Knowledge that all beings possesses, from birth [similar in possessive intelligence] a knowledge that has no needs to be learnt or discovered by man. NOTE TO WORLD: For god is god, and man is man-for such a "title" remains onto the differ and can never be misinterpreted but many such as a "title" has been misused by mankind. For man rethinks to the inhabitant of an intelligent brain though little to the extent, that an intelligent man can never finish what he creates, for such a creation survives only when the future rated minds continues such a pursuant works are completed and praised upon, for the most praises goes to the knowledge of the one who have discovered such a knowledge and little goes to the "continual one" who have vested, their intelligence, to finish another beings creation, in the present times, where such as their knowledge, can be better used to combat all feats at their present era's. And to this a mans feats becomes dangerous when the minds of the past have not created any inventative knowledge to any survival improvements to better themselves at such era and era's to come. To whatever a person does, a person must do it with great 'honor' and 'dignity'-no matter what a feats are. Due to such honor comes accomplishment-while the infidelic ones bask under such accomplishment, creating their own system out of the hardship of others, to these infidels are the utmost "critics" to endeavours, created by those who lurks for Improvements to their survival. To these critics can do no better but feel the burden and mocked all saying and turn their heads to all reasoning.

REVEALATION: Politicians do their jobs by introducing all the glamour of their nation and their existing laws that they have created but never unfold their systems capability in effecting its strength unto the citizens. For the citizens is where all efforts government take its last stand. Citizens do their job by securing their safety and knowing their limits and boundaries and survival is what brings them to their fullest capabilities. And the flags and the history behind the flag and the struggles to create as their system are.

A KABUL OF FLAGER PATRIOTISMS for FOREIGN INTERVENTIONISTS

There is no patriotism in searching for freedom from foreign interventioners nor is it an act of kabulment working for such interventionists—where successors becomes losers and the losers becomes winners.

For the world as we know it, our allies becomes our lethal "combatants" and our "combatants becomes our searching hope for an ally.

{a}For be aware our allies knows all our secrets and our endeavours.

{b}For our allies bedded in our camps and spoke little of their achievements but ask more from the host nation who searches for a friend-not any special friend but one who seemingly spies for his benefits and the benefits for others.

{c}For our allies witness our strategies and our intelligence as a people and as a societal strength, knows our weakness in our defenses.

{d} For our allies knows what we drink for our thirst and eat for our hunger-for our allies knows all of what we do but little is told about them. So hosts, when hosting never bother to ask or hinder why the secrecy. Continue to not bother because he is amongst friends, who have witnessed all planned attacks.

{e}For our allies can corrupt any developments.

"Comradeship" for such a word is never in existence-you stand alone. Every nation to itself. To if such a nation has leaders that possesses fear, then be warned about being conquered by rival nations, to this fear can be contagious, to master it, can bring courage to, to the situate\ion at hand.

BEWARE OF WHAT YOU MAY OF CONQUERED-FOR OTHERS WILL SEARCHED HEARTILY FOR IT-FOR WHAT IS YOURS, BELONGS TO YOU AND YOUR PREDESSORS AND SUCH A TREASURE MUST BE FOUGHT FOR AGAINST THOSE WHO LURKS FOR IT.

BRAIN PUZZLE: A THEOROLOGICAL IDEA TO RENDER UNTO

-A fearful man shoots a courageous man 100 times, thinking that such a man was a "superhuman"-and the courageous man who believes he is a superhuman "himself' shoots a fearful man 100 times because he thought his life was a threat to him-

So in all logic the fearful man was actually shooting a 'super human' but such a superhuman cannot be less of a human, one must have special attributes but in the real of the world was only a mere thought, purported by a "courageous man" who believes he is a super human in thought only. To these two men are considered to be "human idealists"-the minds of some men thinks in one level, inherit all feats other men creates and basks in its presence, while others think abnormally and inherit nothing but slander and condemnation from others who do not know or cannot explain such a development. And to this is why both men were tested for their nature of intelligence.

How a fearful man can shoot a man 100 times because he thinks such a man possesses supernatural strengths, so as the other man. To both these men exhibit some sort of fearfulness but in different ways, it makes no sense unless both men are the same man, trap in disillusionment. For such people in the world do endeavours in participation to their enriched life for accomplishment. To these two, undoubtedly are a example of the mecca of understandability on how the simple human can go through depths of ideas and become trap in such ideas that all relations that deals with the society becomes null and void.

OR IS IT-That the fearful man shoots a man because such a man was a courageous man. The fearful man done such a act because his overwhelmed fear stirred him more fear of becoming courageous, thus making such a act of shooting a courageous man, but unnoticeably by the fearful man, he has committed an act of courage.

The courageous man shoots a man because such a man was a fearful man. Such an act was done because he found that the fearful man was a contagious threat to his life by introducing "fear" into him, due to his ideals of being superhuman.

Unnoticeably by the courageous man an act of "fear" instill such an action to be done. In both cases what both men lacks they have gotten supernaturally without asking by their "unseen emotions". OR IS IT: That one man became two men, due to this separation, one man possesses the emotions of "fear" and the other "courage". During their lives they parted ways resulting in major catastrophic development. Due to such development both emotions meet their final destinations. So different they have become unnoticeably they have become, they start shooting at each other thus resulting one recognized that the man with "fear" needed "courage" to do an act and the man with "courage" needed "fear" to do an act.

To this man finally understood the importance of both the emotions he is in possession with.

TERRORRISTS NETWORK AFFILIATIONS

Have to do with up scaled dangerous system in place to survival any continual existence of their idea to the real of the world. Know wonder such network cannot be discovered whether unspoken by the society that hides such an individuals movements or either such individuals made a great decision to be outcast out of the governance of policy makers.

WHAT IS THIS SYSTEM: This system only survives at its initial stage and furtherance when the human figure dominates it when such minds introduce ideas and to these ideas must be attained and controlled and harness by those who desire to approach and capture its strength for means of patriotism or survivalism. Only when participation is seen only then the idea also called the system survives amongst man. When nonparticipant are shown the existence becomes useless and ineffective thus introducing the "citizens" to create their own system which may be off disapproval to all existent laws created by the existing "government"

Some participate to the existing government but create their own system at intervals towards the existing entity. Sectorialisation is when the system becomes divided in opinion thus the creation of "faction groups" which can come as citizens arm factions, government instituted representatives arms, foreign interventionists arm. And to this, those who belongs to no affiliated groups becomes tragic target, if such factions use violent behavior to further their cause.

SUPPORT ARM: To what was created before is not what are seen today for too many educators have captured what was created by honest idealists, whose intentions was to be powerful in a remote situation, where the individual was not amongst great men but common men with little endeavours. To after years have been evolved so have mankind ideas, until now where today we are the most powerful beings the world have ever seen due to what has been accomplished.

MY INTELLIGENCE WHICH BECOMES A SYMBOL OF MY SKILLS SHALL BE BESTOWED UPON AS MY "PAINT BRUSH" AND THE OPPONENT BECOMES MY "PAINT" AND THE RESULTS BECOMES MY "PICTURE".

Or what a beauty shall it be such surrounds of such bleeding heart-the victor and the victorless.

BEARANCE—OF—ARMS

What we are about to embark in are the forgotten words of a lost idealist, educator, philosopher way of thinking, a way forgotten by intelligent minds of creators of governments and creators to its existence with those who accepts its existence within generations of mans independence to function. In any type of functional government all citizens are privy to freedom even those who accepts a discipline life of "enforcers of rule". Who creates such rules-which in turn represents embodied systems. The system that have the will and power to "bear arms" the uniforms. Occasionally some citizens who possesses no desire to represent no system has "arms" themselves but use of such arms becomes useless but yet effective in times of need—perhaps time of descion making policy. But yet citizens are also privy to freedom without fear or just prejudicial cause, perhaps flaunting, showing or misinterpreting the representation of the use of arms and ammunition may prove to be volatile within the eyes of regular living citizens. Taunting can create a living hell to those who misrepresents the functions of a system and what it stands for to act with accordance in keeping the peace within any important substantial society gathering with or without relevance of heavy artillery. Remember that citizens that are classed, divided can become potent groups of people Citizens-People who represents all aspects of the affairs of nation, may it be for better relations or for striving difficulties.

Criminal citizens-Noted as {creative idealist in their rightful placing} are people who have been branded a name within a system which follows order, they are open minded people who take it upon themselves to create their own laws within a already existing system. And to this when these two entities coincide, devastation occurs. The system which responds to these new types of laws, exercise their power to constrain such, if failures arise, politicians then find foreign interventionists to help create a new existing law.

Authoritative citizens-People who are appointed by the subordinates of ranks to exercise all means necessary to control the general public for the greater good of the country.

Public servant citizens-Are people who posses skills to contribute for the public interests, this system represents part of the authoritative but on their part "bear no arms".

Foreign citizens-Persons who represents their intellects and knowledge of business to do trade amongst other economies. Such person are privy to all access available to them but others might exercise stringent measures about certain developments within their securities.

COMMANDING PLEDGES

WHEN ALL IS LOST, TRUST IN YOUR INSTICT TRUST IN WHAT YOU BELIEVE-FORGET ALL WHAT OTHERS MAY SAY, AT THAT POINT YOU MAY NEED TO HEAR WHAT THEY HAVE TO SAY AND LISTEN CAREFULLY WHAT THEY "MEAN" TOO SAY-FOR ALL IS NEVER LOST-TRUST WHATS WITHIN YOU AND NOT WHATS OUT THERE WITH YOU.FOR ALL THAT IS OUT THERE-FOR ALL YOU CAN SEE-IS NOT ALWAYS WHAT IT MEANS. ALL WHAT THEY THINK THEY BELIEVE-FRIENDS THEY WANT

TO BE-ENEMIES THEY HOPE TOO ACHIEVE, CHALLENGE THEY PRAY TO SEE, WHEN YOU DON'T TRUST WHAT YOU BELIEVE TO THIS YOU THEN BELIEVE, WHAT OTHERS SAY TO ACHIEVE-HOW TO ACHIEVE-WHEN TO ACHIEVE-YOUR MIND THEN CONCIEVE BITTERLY—PRODUCT OF INSANITY, THEN ALL BECOMES LOST, TO END SUCH A COST, ONE MUST NOT SEEK TO MUCH OF ANOTHERS BELIEFS-THIS TRAIT OF DISBELIEFS. WARNING TO THOSE WHO ARE WEAK-WEAK IN MIND WEAK IN BODY, THOSE WHO CRAVE FOR KNOWLEDGE, FROM EVERYBODY, SOMEBODY, NO BODY-ask a question "ARE YOU MY BUDDY?"

Give action to what you believe, and you shall, you see, to Achieve the similar equality of beliefs, as if asking another For same of beliefs. "Kiss them and love them for they are my own"

CHAPTER V

UNIFORM AND SOCIETY

NOTE: The police system can become a military system, when they abandon their function as guardsmen for the people and develop a training method about the portfolio of just enforcement of laws to honorsmen of the state.

NOTE: The society today, one cannot differentiate between the police a civilian-to this a civilian creates an authority for themselves and the police who are appointed authority by the heads of government recognize this strength no more than a job and to this authority finds a more suitable opponent to gather its strength and to this it finds it way to the very corrupt minds of any citizens, no matter their variable functions within their responsible "sectors". "The one life to live responsible" response, they give those who shyly represents its continual function likewise between ordinary good civilians and the ordinary citizens who represents the arms of the government by power of will and not by choice. To this is why within any government arm building, a civilian must respect its function it represent within the society and one shall not disrespect it in any way-or—to this is a arm of the government, the building you see, these uniform you see-respect it for what you seem it too be. To every one are citizens but when responsibility comes when civilian citizens are creating a system of their own, when retaliated action and words are shown for the littlement function.

TO ACHIEVE A FREE MINE COMMANDING PLEDGE

To achieve—the believe, this great entity-of one's man Ephany-this solemn we free-this man you called-"greed" All Apollo's creed-all anthems read—that makes me deal With great supreme-behold my power of stripany-signal to Succeed, the mind rest freely-when this becomes achievable Then and only then such actions becomes "unreal". The level Of thought and idea becomes more than the average man can Achieve.

A CONTROL TONGUE ALWAYS KEEPS A WISE HEAD

SOCIETAL WARFARE

Societal warfare {1} :Once before and said and will continue, beware and be warn that civilians in a democratic run nation are considered to be powerful, so shall such civilians will show no remorse, if indeed they understand the freedom of movements, they shall harness its strength of laws and use it against the "governing laws"

Intimidation-Has a lot of meaning too it. To intimidate or taunt someone's feeling to do what you desire in retrospective view to a system.

Intimidate-To intimidate persons who possesses no form of strength or desire, to rule but makes up certain strength of persons within certain sectors-division-place. Or whom are amongst those who wishes to be corrupt against governing system, walks amongst them but their intentions are not concentrated or similarity are shown similar to those who can.

To this it means that not every civilian that opposes all systematic laws and who shows it at time s are not trying or attempting to destroy its existing functions to exercise it powers equally.

Intimidate-To intimidate means that the uniforms that are warned by such individuals, intimidates all understanding of morality and equality. The uniform begets their better judgement to function correctly and to this the civilians themselves can exercise that intimidation into fearful acts and then becomes courageous cheers to create actions that are soldierists.

Societal warfare {2} When an existing controlive government loses all controlive powers over its people by dominated factions which exists from no other than its population who seems to have different views of control measures upon them, there can be no longer a "government" it then becomes a battlefield for ownership of such a nation. But the system which surrounds existingly, still is in existence but not wholly, such influence extents due to factions, separation of the land.

Societal warfare {3} To this knowledge about destabilization, in formalities to governance, is relativity important to representatives of a system functioning in the real of the world. And to this there can never be a government where sectorialization never exists.

NOTE: For man, there will always be those who pronounce themselves as strong and after such pronouncement-they shall fight for the weak with appraisal for themselves. Their, shall also be those who pronounce themselves as weak and after such pronouncement shall hide amongst the strong. For such traits are common within the system of mans interventions.

POWERS OF THE ARMY THAT SOELY CONSTITUE

The military system is the only system that can create a system outside any government regime and such influential powers to destroy, combat and pulverize any competition, whereas the police system, so highly recognized by many government institution of parliamentarians bodies can only show such effectiveness within the land, it represents and governs and not outside any system. Such as the judiciary it represents. Even if such systems holds powers of arrests, these creative ideas shall not last forever, for such as civilians who sees the ideas of constitutional rights and freedom of rights, are recognized by the eyes of the beholders {civilians} as non essentials to what they believe. To such beliefs are the system they create called "soldierrisms" to "survivalists". For the police system represents the law that governs civility whereas the army constitutes their own system by the creation of others. For the army shall not run its strength by the ideas of one leader, may it be a member of such system or a chosen one by vote of the nation on one dominant ruleship.

WARS OF THE UNIFORMS 1

What does it take to wear and bear the uniform. The uniform are a representation of a existence system and nothing else. When civilians take up matters in their own hands and disrupts those that wears uniform, they are also disrupting the good will of a good governing body-hence the same with the system of governance jurisdictions over all systems including the justice system. These appointed judiciary servicemen and women are neither, survivalists or idealists, their functions are to, conform with the laws created and make judgements to is conformities.

But when there are forces, created to destroy or hamper the uniform and their functions then such persons that were meant to wear such uniforms are bracketed to only using an opportunity as just a 'job" but to other democratic nations, or other bearance of it, it's more than a job, it's an opportunity to serve a nation and represents its boldness and effectiveness, through any danger internally and foreign invaders externally or both.

"Civilians must know their place"-it's not just a rented suit-its loyalty to country and fellowmen, loyalty to yourself, to understand discipline and freedom of oneself-"survival" Uniform is survival-all those that wear it, are not just simple beings but superior and always ready for a battle or war.

{the uniform is a representation of the government, when civilians, citizens disrespects the uniform, they are also disrespecting the government}

WARS OF THE UNIFORMS 2

When a foreign invader, invades a nation territorial borders and such nation is no longer capable to withstand such resting developments, such invading uniforms has the authority to create a new government, under such battorial nations conquests. The destroyed system includes the laws of independence, republic status and their governing laws, which therefore consists the controlment of the uniforms, which becomes powerless, due to such uniforms and those who bear arms to it, has no more, a body too command after. So the uniform and to those who that bear arms to it have befall their authority and are now prisoners of war Or in the sense civilians to a fallen empire, if escaped, separatisms they shall be named—{bearing arms to fight for a lost fallen system and their destroyed independence}. Ownership goes to the belligerent conquering nation.

Overthrownment of the governing body of a country, land mass, nation: This is where a group of civilians, foreigners, uniform officers take evasive action to control the persons involve in law and order and the creation of the rulement, in order to have discussions or after discussions, on matters both the governing body and the group in interest cannot agree on.

MILITARTY INVENTIONS NOW A FASHION STATEMENT IN THE WORKING WORLD

For we have witness that all inventions created by mankind in the past, are within our doorstep. Who would of believe that a university teacher, educating the eager student about quantum physics, nuclear divisions, divided enough to be used on domestic instruments for energy, which at a time, no less than a century ago, was hid away by powerful nations, thus the continual creation of spies and spying agencies open their closet experimentation. The telephone to cell phone, to advance technological advancement in training defense warfare. These advancements were first subject to military use, before the general public uses such an idea to become a fashion statement, making the "dollar" more convenient in its statue among the world's elevated economies.

THE PARADING OF UNIFORM IN RANKS

{1} Having ranks has nothing to do with seniority, the higher the ranks, the more they rally the cowardice, bravery have nothing to do with seniority, it's you the soldier have manage to hide when friend lees taking crossfire, come home a big star.

{2}Having ranks have nothing to do with being, good looking, the higher the ranks the ugly they are.

{3} Having medals branded on their chest, how pretty they may be, have nothing to do with comradeship, parading uniforms, disassembling on a show, collecting lost memories, called them memos.

{4} Having a army, have nothing to do with being powerful, the greater the army, the lesser the skills, "pour more water than blood".

{5}Having true democracy have nothing to do with being a stable enterprise, the division of powers causes more blood than water. {6}Having a firearm have nothing to do with surviving, only cowards pull the first trigger, non-inventors take pride to which is not their own. {too much non-inventors, non idealists in this world, too much taking pride to which is not their own}

SOLDIERRISM AND THE ABILITY TOO SURVIVE THE INDEPENDENCE

Everyone wants to be a soldier, everyone wants to be grasps power, may it be within the framework of societal gangs or for totalatarisms, over a nation. What sense does it have for a mass of country, occupied by people to decide on being independence. Whether all independence was fought by warfare and hidden by doctrines of the creation of political science, how to rule a mass variety of disillusioned human beings. When there is war, which is covered by some political scheme. To what happens to a nation invaded by foreign interventionists, do all have to pay for paul. Each individual has the ability to survive own their terms, depend not only on the framework of persons deployed to some, the very existence of such governments in times of warfare. Independence to one self, knowing that I determine where my life goes and determine where my life goes, and dictated by some leaders agendas for power struggle. That is true independence, if there are two million people living in a nation, and to this all have acquired independence of themselves, destroying the differentiated bond, the nation would be strong and difficult to brake.

A system of controlment falls when there are opposition and to such opposition, who sees the weak links annihilates it to its very core.

One all-think all-be all-fall all-no one is spared. That is what independence is of a nation, independence of the individual first. There are many organization, coalition, movements that are created within the frame work of mankind inventitive systems we called "government". The more they separate the world systems, the more would world war be near. The civilians that bear arms against the rule of the land, forcing the creation of separatists and those civilians who trust the rulement of the system but are corrupted in their ways, then the civilians that wants nothing and hopes for the best, take note to unfavourable civilians way of living, it takes 10% overally within he collection of stable governments in the world.

AFFIRMATION: DON'T SEEK BEHIND THE MASK-WHEN YOU SEEK NOT TO WEAR IT-BUT—SEEK BEHIND IT, FOR IF LIFE HAS CHOSEN YOU TO BE ONE OF THE "FEW" AND THE "BRAVEST" OF MANY-AND MAY CIRCUMSTANCES APPEAR-DO IT FOR ANY. WE DO WHAT WE WANT TO DO-WILLINGLY KNOWING, THE PRICE OF DOING.SO-SEEK BEHIND THE MASK, WHEN SEEKING TO WEAR IT-THE BEARER MUST TAKE IT FIT TO SEE THROUGH IT.

PATRIOTISM: To love a country is indeed wonderful, to its creative systems and its effectiveness and the way how human being create ideas to improve such status can be an act of "patriotism"

CHAPTER VI

RELATION OF MAN'S WORLD AND MAN'S EXISTENCE

Governmental arms—There exists these correctional institution or policing institutions due to that citizens cannot have power over themselves. This idea comes from the intelligent behavioral manner of human beings at the utmost distinguish, investigative medium throughout history. To this idea was written and noted and precautionary measures were undertaken to prevent these behaviours in control of any types of government but some has the power to infiltrate due to powerful citizens, who were respected by the entire "citizens arms". The governmental arms which are chosen by the citizens arms which in all, consists of the entire nation of people of any institutions or arms or position. But to the contrary without any citizens arms there can never be, no other arms in relation to a good government due to that you need these systems to be filled by non other by the decision of the citizens. Governmental arms cannot control, no matter what type of enforcement towards citizens arms. These citizens are the only type of citizens arms that can destroy all or any type of defiant system they are trying to create in existence that corruptly plagues the government and judiciary functions, these creative destroyers of the system.

INTELLIGENT BEHAVIOUR.

BEHAVIOUR OF THE MIND

This behavioral pattern comes about when information is being feed to the brain or mind and to this the "brain" reacts intelligently and behaviorally alongst without the important elements that sustains within the body. Nourishment to provide the continuation of the use of the brain. Conclusively when information is being feed, the brain reacts in a behavioral manner but unlike the physical behavioral manner of the structures within the body that creates a different "reaction" but the assistance of the brain to determine if the reactions are real. To create this, a different type of information is inhibited, creating a variable behaviour from the body to indulge the brain to respond with senses in full alert. Emotional behaviours—This type of behaviour has definitely no connections with the body's structures within the behaviours that are shown out of the body which are caused by the disturbtion of the impulse of the major brains thinking in logic judgement which then causes the uncontrolled reactions of the body.

THE NEW VS THE OLD

The existence is there, it is real it is present, it has been created from the unreal thought and ideas of mans intelligence. We become it and we live from it but what if another system has been developed, not to destroy its continual existence but to coincide in its harmony but these creators of such existence would doubt its continual harmony and demise a planning attack. To this is when an existence or any creation out of the depths of the mind, it is to safeguard the maker from the existence superior of the combined system.

How can they destroy what they cannot see-to the source of the system does not lie within the great structures that employ their superior power over man, which are operated by the same man who knew little or nothing about the ideas that lies within the brain of the true inventors that persuaded these inventative minds to perform their actions that hence created these ideas to reality and contain the stamina and superior strength to live, corrupt, breathe amongst the very relationship of man today, tomorrow and the futureated.

CRIME: Is a word created when two or more individual human beings gets into a argument creating an entity of one or both humans beings has resulted in death by the competition without one deciding on walking away. Crime cannot be destroyed, here two emotional beings creates a dominating force of massive adrenaline actions that results in not thinking about the consequences until the final actions are entirely terminated.

TYPES OF COUP-E-TAT

{1} Military personnel refuse to work dependently in the existing system thus introducing a "coup"

{2} Military personnel join a "civilians" arms group" to introduce a "coup"

{3} A "citizens arms group" introduce a "coup"

{4} A citizens arms group introduce a "coup" towards the existing government with the assistance of "foreign intervention"

{5} Foreign interference introduce a "coup" illegally-after debating diplomatically or not or of non participating in any talks on creating a system that can introduce freedom of rights towards the people who resides in the trouble nations.

When citizens holds the power of the nation by force, by introducing a system against the governing masses, and by these inventive, citizens use to their advantage all the disgust their previous system had in place.

MACHINES AND NON MACHINES

Ages has occur when we have become more dependently on the "machines" due to its functionable attributes, that can do mans work or duties as a man but more efficiently and at a more adaptable enormous amount of strength and capability.

God created the world

God created human beings

Man is created in reference to both man and woman

Man created thoughts and ideas and their constant overuse too evolvement to defend the harshness of the world.

Man created machines, machines of all types and functions-created by all types of intelligent being throughout the history of mankind.

Non machines-A very powerful affordable opponent towards the invention of machines. Mans other inventions are the ideas and the principles that are seen throughout the mecca of history, where a new type of machine evolves powerfully to all extended limits on all locations on earth. The intelligence to rule many or a lot of human beings at one or many locations by one supreme or chosen entity by the people that encircles such place or "civilization". Where the intelligent mind encompasses at one source. This is called "government"-a machine as well but its functions do not depend well on maintenance but of interference of governance but it only survives well on dependencies and willingness of the people who have chosen such an entity.

To this we can say that without prejudice that all the machines are powered and operated by "human beings" who have been bestowed to its function of operation. Those beings chosen or took such machines are not inventors of such or inventors of new ideas but just "holders" of such development until some intelligent supreme idealist decide otherwise.

NOTE TO WORLD: An idea are meant for one person for another indifferent mind to keep such an idea to survive-one must accept its unique principles-to when adapted to it-your ideas would be in vain. These types of ideas are mostly seen in governance and in rulement over people. To these ideas were not invented in these times but of times before, to the man of yesterday-its survival depends on man acceptance to it, not withstanding they themselves hold ideas of their own. "Why do they adopt these ideas of other men and leave behind their own ideas-the man of today?" Human beings are liberated by bondage but not ideas-their self image are more important than their personal privilege to create ideas during their era of reignment. For genre to genre one idea is stuck within the spectrum of the mind to those who want to capture the most powerful system man has ever created-"politics". To the military which supposedly can be the ever powerful gets between the disgusts of politics and decision are made without consultation. All of this system may have never been in the existence in the world during a utmost long period of time-was it for ones man ideas to bring forth an idea to the realness amongst man.

NOTE: Man has used all his power to create an existence out of his intelligenated mind-an existence spoken off are the secrets surrounding mans efforts and triumphs, these secrets are sometimes discovered by extrodinary beings-beings themselves create their own system, that the "real" and the felt of human emotions and surrounds the individual during their triumph of success, seems to not understand the basics towards what makes the world so unique. To this after discovering such ideas that penetrates their minds during the process of elimination of the super real to the process of the unreal. The gifted mind of such supreme beings then undertake to its final discovery of telling the rest of the world to which they only live by one rule-a rule of understanding all elements that pertains to their riches, to which becomes a slave to their measures.

To this is why the world will now learn of the gifted mind who penetrates all available doubts that man can explore further that the "real" unto the "unreal", where readily information are waiting for those who searches for its truth-by means of device used to inhibit stimuli of knowledge thus giving them the additional strength. But more ideas are invented for war than the possibility to gain more information on the bodies' defences or possibility of new life elsewhere other than earth. "More to fund for war—more to gain after such war"

"PARTICIPANT" & "PARTICIPATION"

{1} Participant—to make rule over others and the world by emotions captured over their own rules to control them-their actions become unlimited top their participation like so others during the genre of the human race.

{2}Non participant-to rule the world but to live by the rules of god and fellowship of god before their times and time to come.

A GOVERNMENT SOLDIER

A government soldier is trained to "survive" his "will" is to "kill" so the same it is towards a non government soldier or regime. On their efforts continuous training and adapted to it rewards the participant urges to survive every battle on the grounds—for this is the "military", your life becomes indebted towards services, to this services are representing the name of your nation and the superiority it holds amongst the people who resides in such nation and the intelligence they may be in possession of.

RELATIONS RELATING TO CREATED INDEPENDENT BODIES AND THEIR EXISTED FUNCTIONS-THUS REMAINING AS CORRESSPONDENCE BETWEEN THE THREE{3}POWERS OF DEMOCRATIC GOVERNMENT RELATIONS.

{1}Parliamentarians, {2}judiciary {3}police system.

To these three powers which ridiculously existed by the creation of a government. To these three powers which are controlled independently by means of an official high ranked person who is presiding over all matters relating to such a power or system. "but can a politician intervene in matters relating to one of these two system". Reluctantly these politicians are destroyed only by the laws they have created, laws pertinent to no abridge evening of such other system. But to this the judiciary is not an international allianced committee where it pops in any creation of a functional government in any part of the world. To when overthrownment occurs within the judiciary it can crossborders. So it is in some democratic citizens thinks in their democracy way.

Powers which are so closely tied, regardlessly if these three systems are independent in their functions there are still closely tied. This means one was created so followed the other, then the other until the three became a replica of themselves. But the human beings in control of instituting some form of rulement are not a genuine replica in the eyes of humanity. Exercising all means to create others powers of superiority by means of a replicated or a new system or a new system existed from the old system, then the system will never increase in power over controlment of the nation, thus resulting in rest of the population who possesses no form of powers within the nation, "creates" a new system which resembles them in ways of either being:

{1} Depressed thus creating a reprisal system
{2} Patriotic thus creating a patriotic system which can be broken down in two, either it be retributed or in good faith.

THERE ARE THREE TYPES OF DREAMS

{1} Dreams of the mind: That has no worthy accomplice with the action of the human who beholds such a strength but creates this dream by usage of the thoughts and ideas of his own brain and not functionally brings it forth to the "real" of the world. This idea dream in real, in existence, once the beholder is still alive in this world but the existence is not real in the presence of man and men.

{2} Dreams of skills: This means a human being may posses a unique skill which is shown to the presence of man and men to their liking but it shown at a time that holds less efficiency and needs the assistance of the "brain" which controls ideas and dreams, in order to succeed its further existence in its strength and power. This does not mean that the human who has such a skill has no dreams, it may be a different dream which may it either be amongst man or not but may have no power of strength to control such other skills.

{3} Dreams in its simple comformities: Which means the "dream" is shown unto man with the introduction of the action of the human being, whose reluctance are to show it for reasons of his own but to the extent the "dream" are not shown entirely amongst men, due to either searching its hidden strength or for purpose to let man in the world to either hear and understand or die with stupidity.

NOTE: For the jobs of a politician are to employ their thoughts and ideas and introduce such an idea to the reality of man—the nation at whole. Occasionally some ideas do not come into the comformities of the real world thus adhering to the citizens of the nation to introduce such a word called "promises". Which each dilemmas are pronunciated. But the citizens depend to much on the shoulders of the government, citizens themselves can institute measures on governing their own selves and how to survive in the 21st century, by employing thoughts and ideas on their own account, therefore introducing two medium of governance, the government and the citizens, to this there can be a balance of information medium being transferred to one medium to the other thus provoking any creation of a gap of non communication like so many government has employed, not forgetting the very most important announcement by such.

NOTE: In any such a government either democratic, authoritative in any demise they come, "politicians" needs to take greater responsibilities for actions done by any entity system they have created-regardless of their "independent" statue or representations. Under the parliamentarians are the justice system and the police system.

The police system as noted highly are a independent body organized by a high ranking officer who in turn, shared such a responsibilities as other shared by the surbodinates. But the importance of such a system are to implement all forms of laws unto the general public whilst others who may not posses a high emotional disturbance of uncontrolled behavoural pattern which likely some people love to create unto such an existence. Their jobs show some form of importance

"To why the disregard of them?"

"To why the banishment of them?"

"To why do they be constantly attacked by the public and the politicians?"

The politicians now and their predecessors have created such a system, to their can be no other force capable to implement such are their written laws.

MANS SUPPORTS HIS BRAIN

Welcome man's world-his "inventions", welcome to man's life his "decisions" and finally, welcome to man's "life span"-his ability to "survive". To all this features represents a human being, whilst being among the living and to the dead. The human being becomes nothing of worth, to the remaining living, but riches and to the non living and the unseen. Welcome to such a world of human being, who posses great potential knowledge in their increase of intelligence amongst man and god; those who possess great knowledge about God and lack great lurking knowledge for wealth amongst man. Those who posses equal amount of knowledge where the world needs such a being assistance during hours of conflict amongst men and decision rests on them. So it depends amongst the conflict but when all are dead, knowledge about god is important and the use of the intelligent brain of man to search for its treasures whilst deciding optional disputes amongst the intervention of the system.

MAN AND MEN

Man-A man is a human being which holds one idea or ideas to compete towards the existing world of men. Man can also be referred to as a man and woman, when speaking on matters of accomplishment each being has created thus referring their ideas must be created and brought forth to the real of the world Men-Men are to describe a collecting of the male species in togetherness or their intelligence if knowledge has been brought to a single point in existence, thus creating a system of collection of ideas, thus creating one source of power. All man associated in this regime thinks alike, thus their goals are the same, thus if a combatant destroys one in meaning, that being has never been destroyed, depending on how many are associated in the regime.
AFFIRMATION: 2 COMBINE "FORCES" PRODUCES A COMBINATIVE "POWER" OF A MIXTURE OF—2 DIFFERENT STRENGTHS OF EQUAL "FORCE"-when the 2 COMBINES, it creates a "POWER" that is not existence, thus creating the word "ENEMY" ENEMY—is broken down to 2-{1}A COMBATOR{2}A DEFEATER-due to their "different strengths" and skills to use" it".

CHAPTER VII

KNOWLDEGE OF ALL ASPECTS OF FIELD OF MANKIND

SEPERATION OF THE SYSTEM OF POWERS

To this we already know, that to all developed existing system comes all sub-eternal system and their separation of powers to existent controlments. The police service job is not only to enforce the law of the land amongst the system but most importantly is too control the creative ideas of civilians and their intrusive power to create ideas for the destruction of non-participant and participants towards their duty. Which is to:

{1} To serve the system
{2} Control internal depress
{3} Defend the honor of independence.

There is no difference between any uniforms, any individual attempts to disrupt such functions can be dealt a serious hand to destruction of their own system.

NOTE {1}: There is no loyalty in "gangsterism". The only loyalty lies to the continuation of an ideal called the "government". This is the true function of true ideas, to follow, to obey and to serve. Where rules and regulation applies. Non can be said towards "gangsterism" or civilians bearing arms for the destruction of self, property belongs to the practice of the system.

BLOOD SPILLS

All forms of system created by mankind has been created by "blood" of the servants called man. Where man follows their ideas, triumph over them, fight for them and allow subjects to continue its survival amongst mankind. To this the 21 St century all changes to be made must be fought and won by the lost of lives, so corrupt our minds have become to which we know little of good will and good thoughts amongst men. To us man digest all good deeds brought to them by good fellowmen and spits out their loathsome behaviour, the man of the future. Creators of what they think, money have been created for the simple ideas that are eye approaching, mouth dropping instruments in today' world. These creative ideas, put to test, have become a battlefield amongst man, to develop more unique powerful structures at all levels of creation All honor and glory to {the idealists, inventors, creators} the ones that wears the uniform. The destruction of the uniform can never be, will never be and will never be thought to be. The destruction of the system will always be once there is separation of the powers that exists within the democratic system. Systemic controlive laws needs enforcement and good patriotic citizens to follow. There can be a lot of factors resulting in good governance, here are a few:

{1} Loyal subjects
{2}Loyal leaders
{3}Technology
{4} Iron fist to retributional attributes to warfare.

THERE ARE FIVE POWERS WHICH REPRESENT A GOVERNMENT

{1} Money that holds the economy for exchange is a representation of the system.

{2} The uniform

{3} The flag, which is a pledge to allegiance

{4} The anthems

{5} The buildings of structure that represent the creation of laws and order of laws.

Inventions and creativity does not amount to a good government, due to inventors can be abused for foreign intimidation. Signs to the beginning of the destruction of the system are the frequent distortion of all five elements and to the inventions, any develop of all that can be maximize to enormous power within an abnormal frequent changes can be signs. Any change in behaviour of these persons holding power within their division

NOTE TO WORLD {2}: There is no loyalty in gangsterism, mafiarisms, separatist's movement because their idea of loyalty is corrupt. What happens when persons appointed in power, becomes corrupt the, uniform takes charge of the situation, literally. The laws of the land can never be destroyed with exceptional, of a fallen government, due to internal continual disturbance or either foreign intervention, namely a "war". But some fundamentals of it remains intact, and this is what all persons appointed to serve, protect the laws of the land must stand and not give way by any internists.

PLEDGE FOR A DIFFERENCE:

BE AS BEST AS YOU CAN BE-AND GOOD AS YOU CAN, FOR CHANGE IS IN EVERYTHING, EVERYONE, ACCEPTANCE FOR IT IS AN DELUSION

BUT A CHOICE TO COME OUT OF THE DARKNESS WITH RENEW STRENGTH TO THE LIGHT OF HOPE, BRILLANCE AND TRUST IN GOD. WILL MAN'S ACCEPTANCE TO FORGE WILL, AMONGST THE GREATER OF MEN-TO LIVE IT, IS THE DIFFER, TO WRITE ABOUT AND HAVE KNOWLEDGE IT WITHOUT EXPERIENCING IT, CAN BE A "DIFFER."

Everyone must live for a change, life is too short, one must not dwell too much with the unacceptance that "fear" is the controller and "tears" of it is just a remembrance to its continual existence. A system is only strong when the individuals are looking for change, the benefaction of themselves and for honor.

Leaders may come and go with their difference on opinion and the freedom of sovereignty but to those who represent the other way must understand that—{represent your country in honor, to this country comes first} this goes to all civilians and uniform lovers, represent your country, representing "leaders" is never in the job description.

"Always remember, civilians are what make the stronghold of a democratic nation, no matter how much accomplishment leaders make outside the spectrum of their domain".

There can be no honor in disrespecting the independence a nation holds, to all nation, which are built on the framework of man's intelligence are susceptible to failure one point or another. Government can be used for the acceptance of brilliance for good works and also for the works of bad-these atrocities that are seen in today's world within the specter of ruleship, cities are plagued with violence and separatisms to rule among man.

MAN OF THE 21ST CENTURY

You can never see me uttering words to the man with their clouded visions, hiding behind, what they say is their shield of embraced power. But to me their domain exercised by the unique inferiorness to understand today does not rest upon one idea but by the exuberance of many that together can be allied to all defences, tactics and energetic behavioral pattern of the common man. You say "barbarism" is a thing of the past but mankind today uses the skills of killing as a mandatory aspect to achieve all goals and dislikes by members who refused authority by them. So educated, so versatile, so unique is mankind today, they build the power, they hold the power but still fail to recognize that "anger begets anger"

OPPOSITION OF THE PEOPLE-GOVERNMENT VS CIVILIANS:

You can see it is very difficult for the human being today to find life-and true meaning to live, whilst there are so many people guided by one principles an ideal. They fight for it, they die for it, they kill for it, they live for its continual existence.

Since we all know, all ideals come with a price. The destruction of a life or living for an ideal that when such persons die and depart, it dies also, "unless" such inhabitants continue its practice. The continual of such practice, means mankind do not think for their own. Where 80% of ideals comes from the ones who shows it and such persons grows an affection for his own, the 20% is only used for "survival". And ways to survive comes with a heavy price to pay-the use of deadly force if necessary. So when we kill a man for his ideas and the practicing of such an ideal, to when depart his body and exercising of it may be no more-but his ideas still remains in the heart to those such man has preach and if shown acceptance for it, such ideas remain dormant within the world, like so others-just plaguing the good ideas of ever remaining or showing.

Ideas only die when those who have been taught, neglects its practice, due to ideas surrounding other ideals or an inhibited one injected in the "learners" How can you stop behavioural patterns in a sector of a society when everyone heartbeats become one and bleeds as one. Where the younger generations are living the same precedents as the old ones, no change what so ever. Much practice must be attended by governments if such wants to see success in the destruction of separatisms of all what the system policies may hold.

Government and governance is much more than just law and order and all must obey to this is man made laws. One must understand "opposition of the people" will always be meant in any type of government and their behavioural pattern must be always carefully be monitored. A system must see and recognize all gliches made before they become an outbreak.

TO WHAT WARRANT AN OPERATION RIGHT WINGER SUPPORTER

To believe in ones work, one needs to believe in their ideas to warrant it and to exercise its power and to this and only to this, shall one become invincible in all attributes. To one don't need to say words of power to make forms of power to dictate actions of power but the way such inhibitor moves or as such his movements must become powerful enough to the lesser minds in action. An operation for a soldier can and will occur anytime or period in time. Whereas such the use of his skills and intelligence would be sharpened, idolized and convicted by those whose it, those who searches for it, those who has it but are afraid to produce its power.

One cannot posses the willing power and not use it, for it is futile and corrupted to let the lesser minds dictate your actions fully. One must be assertive in their actions and believe in their actions to this is how one learns.

THE LONGITIVITY OF THE LESSER MIND VS THE PRODUCTIVITY OF THE GREATER MIND VS THE WISDOMIC FEW THAT POSSES INFINITE POWER TO RULE, THE WORLDS HUMAN FIGURE, VS THE MIND.

THE COLLECTION OF MINDS: When one has attained true infinite power one must search out to find a worthy opponent, within his field or elsewhere. To combat the mind with the use of creative ideas, created by such or those learnt by others and destruction of the mind can also be attained by:

{1} Creating a conversation in your field-to this one must possess all knowledge in all fields of great intelligence.
{2} Direct or redirect focus on intellectual conversation to your field of work thus dominating every action of thought such opponent may introduce.
{3} Conversate boldly and with reassurance that you know a lot.
{4} Make them believe what you are saying, final conqueringment is shown when the opponent searches for advice or asks a question relating to their field of intelligence or yours.

"What is field of intelligence?"

Field of intelligence is what we humans see everyday, the field of work a human being has use all his brain cell and energy to become, making the result that are witnessed today-a doctor a lawyer are some professions. To these fields are the creation and the relation to continual existence to governance of a country. This is called using your intelligence for the system works, whereas others, the ones that are given names by their cunning works, the separatisms, terrorisms, using their ideas for selfdom gain and not for the continual existence of the system, more or less the destruction of the system.

So the use of the mind in many fields whereas there are others that posses intelligence in many fields, therefore introducing creative ideas to benefit the continuous existence to fields of ideas. The more a person's ideas are put forth to such fields, the more they survive-the lesser minds.

THE DOMINATION OF THE MINDS: One can dominate any minds once those who possesses lesser infinite power, then bow down entirely, their use of their brain. This intimidation then resides "outerly" to the combative fields of a nation status in the framework of the dependency of "power ruling".

To all these words describes the minds of man. The collection of all types of ideas created by the minds of every human being within the network of living species whether ideas be big or small. Destructive or constructive, for the greater future or the existing future.

FOREIGN ELEMENTS: Foreign elements can be introduced within any system in two ways:

{1} For the benefactor of the continual existence of the system, may it be the introduction of the ideas and thought both "masterfully" within their brains but more likely become a disasters within be different network of systems or within technology that seems to be ever growing on industry that generates "great minds" of the future.

{2} The illegal entry made possible by the systems power hunger individuals or the uncontrolled border entry made possible by the civilians or such individuals who possess the power to create diversions.

"Where does the local elements comes in?"

When can the system powerhouses believe that sometimes the answer lies within the structure of the people and their possessive ideas if not one then put many to make one idea because "CHAOS"-within any system is "big business". The leaders at all end needs them, for their finger tips snatching. Why would leaders hold conversation with elements that are destroying the framework of an existing system and encourage its existence by introducing odd jobs to them with substantiated funds, that are in possession of such "extortionists"

CHAOS IS BIG BUSINESS, POLITICIANS ACCEPTS ITS EXISTENCE WITHOUT ANY THOUGHT OR IDEA THAT "TWO HEADS OF POWER CANNOT BE IN ONE ROOM NOR CAN IT BE EASY TO DESTROY".

Individuals that accepts separatisms, terrorisms anarchy cannot divert from such, even the nation leaders introduce ways to divert their attention to destructive creative ideas that such may have tendency for thus the behaviour pattern of separatists beings would remain the same unless otherwise introduce by an inhibitor. There are those who accepts governance and those who accepts anarchy away too good governance-this is noted by their behaviour pattern to the "workforce plenty" of the citizens.

{1} A man who studies separatisms

-Many who fuels separatisms

-A community who is define as separatists.

-A society who lives on being defiants of good behaviour to rule and laws thus introducing their own "methodology" on separatisms.

Their can be a differentiated ratio to government bodies and their agencies against the bodies of separatists. It depends on all aspects

{1}Man power on both ends

{2} Technology on both ends

{3}Funding on both ends

{4} Trust on both ends-to believe in one's beliefs, that is not their own or cannot be.

One body of separatists can be made for a "battlefield" such battlefields can be anywhere, anytime against the two dependant bodies sometimes "non—participants" get between the two and chaos are seen. Many bodies in one area is called a "minefield" sometimes a minefield has civilians or either non-participants living in such esteem abodes. Where the battle does not goes out the outerims of the territory, knowing a battle can come any day, anytime.

TERRITORIAL BATTLEFIELDS: Is either government bodies or separatists fighting for an area that can be potential to either or "causes to their claims"-many bodies in different area is called a "strategic placing for a war"-no matter how domesticated it could be, known as "sectorial battlefield". Where different sectors is also associated with different tactics.

Causes to their claims: Is a definition use in warfare-there must be a reason why such entities at war would love to claim such.

RULE SHIP AND LAWS CREATED BY MAN FOR MANKIND 1

As seen over the years, many manmade creation of types of government no matter, destroyed, converted or either still in existence does not show any reality to the hidden facts, "name and justice" for a name that man themselves are the controller of their own devine power to attributal ruleship-emotions over created laws always and would be the devine power of ruleship.

Democratic rule: A type of favourite ruleship amongst the world today but as seen notably, practice of such seems limitless. The obscurities are seen very transparent over stepping, overtrampling by leaders of power over their man made laws either, created by them, themselves or of the periods before by politics of the past.

Boundaries politics: Has power only to the territorial boundaries that consent the citizens as such-whereas, International politics: As seen notably by their conferences but do they practice this form of democracy when invading such nation. As seen-all forms of war begins by the "breaking of treaty" a consigned signatures that if ever broken can be devasting to the other-no matter what the formation of such a signature could imply

{1}Economical distress
{2} Economical growth
{3}Resources

As seen today a lot of nations break such treaties for untamed reasons, so fragile they are, when such deals with close ties-border control, territorial control. A treaty can be made for the better or the worse which whereby such leaders also include the harm or protection of all citizens of a nation.

CRIMINALS AND CRIME

Criminals-crime can only be made mention towards system existence and not to "religion", for religious warfare is a different cause of war. Criminal thrives on what the system posses:

{1}money

{2}weapons

{3} lifestyle

{4} rights

{5} fuctioning system

NOTE: In a system, for an individual to not have governmental studies or the adaptation to learn what the government beholds are not considered to be unintelligent, positions in a system or workwise has nothing to do with intelligence.

Credentials has nothing to do with intelligence is just the adaptation to learn-to discover the depths of information {to exercise the use of the brain}. Government positions, or to fill these vacancies within the network of the system depends on credentials, without the use of any, such individuals would ultimately use a new form of intelligence in reprisal of what is considered to be intelligence in a system. So behold these individuals would create something of their own, their efforts is shown, whether the forces that detect creativity, sees such action and reacts. Failure of the forces to detect and control the elements created by these new "geniuses" would be futile of them to continue that way and to this is how "separatisms" is created-from a individual to a group, to a society, to a people, to a country. Also it tells how a system is controlling its people creativity.

After all is said-do you think religion leaders can influence the minds of these idealists.

The purpose of these leaders are to are to allow the human beings and their counterparts to search for enlightment to god.

NOTE {1} One of the greatest risks of creating a system is that the citizens has to ensure that their creative ideas goes towards the continual existence of the system from generations to generations. The intelligent masses, is what holds the foundation of a government.

NOTE: {2} When civilian or citizens finds other means to survive, other than what the system bestow unto them such civilians uses the playground of society to fuel their fire. Society is destroyed, the forces who has to react to such elements has to seek ways to keep their families from harms reach.

NOTE {3} It is ever so seen that civilians allow their governing individuals to think for them, allowing them to decide their actions. So weak are their minds and to use it makes it a profitable attempt by these governing bodies to use their defects and so as such to abuse their power.

NOTE {3} A system police service cannot change a "situation" by just arresting all citizens for the breaking of their "laws". To this will never change, the fact states, this is within the spectrum of human behaviour. The will to be defiant, it is within us and to this the real change, then comes about by introducing new method of thinking to the citizens to deeper broader their minds to believe that the system cares.

PLEDGE TO ALLEGIANCE

I AM IN NO WAY INTERESTED WITH AN INTELLIGENT BEING LIFE'S STORY OR CRENDENTIALS-I AM IN EVERY WAY INTERESTED WITH SUCH INTELLIGENCE STORED WITHIN THE FRAMEWORK OF THE MIND-TO SHARE ITS INTELLIGENCE-TO HAVE CONVERSATIONS ABOUT IT-TO ACKNOWLEDGE WHO IS THE "GREATER".

THERE CAN ONLY BE TWO-to these two, there can be those who uses their intelligence inventions for the good of man, and those who does it for the benefits of themselves. To these two is why the world today benefits us all.

OCCUPATION TO DISASTEROUS IDEALS

There can be many ways a system can be destroyed as notably seen by many entities in the world today. Two very well known tactics are

{1} The destruction of heads of government

{2}The destruction of society governance.

{a}Many separatists destroys heads of governments in a means of desperation-by means of controlment-by means of embracing status of power in order to destroy the lesser entities of a system.

{b}The destruction of societal governance-some separatists destroy a society and not heads of government-by means of introducing "chaoticy" amongsts the citizenry in order to panic the heads of government in erratic behaviour not norm to a system. Some separatism introduce creative ideas of anarchy, everyday in new ways or sometimes double-which causes the life of citizens to be stressful. And to this force can be a challenging one due to these separatists who hides amongst the citizenry driving their occupation to disastrous ideals.

THE INTEL

There are two forms of intelligence known or known to few of men

{1} Progressive intelligence

{2} Possessive intelligence

Progressive intelligence-Is the form of intelligence us human live by as by birth till death-our progressiveness to learn new things every day, no matter our positions here on earth represents.

Now-progressive intelligence use in the intellectual format of a government and its governing institution is represented in two{2} domain

{1} Where the citizens of a nation uses their intelligence for the betterment or to fill the many vacancies, that exists within a system. Members of societal efforts.

{2}The citizens that uses another form of education unlike what the government institute, find demeanor ways to survive, a chaotic way of living, where creatisms is rapid and the destruction of the system can be failed to protect its societal lectures in their every field.

Then there are those that are societal people worthy to the system but uses the benevolent weakness of their counterparts to fuel chaos for their own personnel demeanors.

Possessive intelligence—Are within the people that contains true wisdomic features like gifted associates to higher power. Prophets then, likewise, there are those who posses infinite sources of power. To all these intelligence, were not taught by anyone or either to the individual, never were they had a keen to learn such as were given by them by birth and to such found its power lying within them.

Sometimes progressive intelligence can be overused by bodies of higher understanding to control all idea, induced and destroy all information stored in the cerebrum, these are considered to be brain washed to be assassins.

THE JOURNEY OF A CIVILIAN IN A DEMOCRATIC SOCIETY

In a system we all began our journey as a "civilian" and end our journey sometimes likewise.

-A civilian in a democratic system is considered powerful and useful at every angle

-A civilian in a democratic system works for the system by means of different ways but their ideals remain "loyal" to the system, building its structures "economically" and its "ideology". So to those of a different caliber of a civilian, those faithful to the system.

{1}High influential civilians-are considered to be "faithful" to the system, those who has authority

{2} Average influential civilians-are considered "loyal" to the system, those who institute authority

{3} Mid average influential civilians-are considered "productive" to the system, those are the ones who possess no form of authority within the system but do posses boundrial authority within their network

{4}Low influential civilians-are considered to be neither faithful, loyal, productive to the systems and to themselves they posses no authority but cunningly attempt to gain authority by means of chaotic behaviour.

To this is note as the "CLASSIFICATION OF CIVILIANS PROGRESS TO SOCIETY IN A DEMOCRATIC ONE"

Purpose of civilians in a democratic society are as follows:

{1} Civilians must in every way use their intelligent mind to better the system in every way.

{2} Civilians must know their place in society, positions do not describe your freedom within the system neither your movements to be controlled.

{3} Civilians must exercise all institute offered by the system.

EDUCATION FROM THE SYSTEM TO THE CITIZENS

Accepted by the civilians or not Civilians who do not accept education of the system are considered "geniuses" in their own way. To live and survive becomes difficult to those who do not adopt. "Can an individual survive within the system without a education, to which this education ensures, such individual gets ajob within the system of work?"-the answer is yes. For mankind over the years make means of adaptation without the use of "governmental enforcement of learning"-called by the name "uneducated mind" by the system, due to not accepting education from the system but deter to mention they are neither.

Unintelligent minds-Within the system, to their intelligence focuses on the ability to combat all measures undertaken by the system. To this intelligence encourages "survival" and improves their methodology to survival. Technology and many ways of getting information, one need not have to enlist in a educational facility but can be taught by an idealist, within their society. And to if such learners have become immune to this form of learning it will become difficult to introduce a new behavioural pattern into such. Sometimes those educated by the system uses their uneducated minds describe in society when all hope is last and immensely provoked their institution in becoming "mules" or slaves to their calling.

Sometimes there can be those who are highly educated in society and use such intelligence to introduce new knowledge created by such to those of uneducated minds, known in society to better their cause.

So, these intelligent minds who are not educated by the system for means of working for the system. Their creative ideas are seen when there, chaotic behaviour or their intelligent scheme is shown in society, to which is to disrupt the continual good will of the system.

So, a system is known as powerful where the governance of its leader has provide every means possible so such citizens can survive, no matter what their influence in the world may be or their world development status, anything other than that-a civilian is likely to create ways to destroy the sanctimony of the citizens to survive.

EMANCIPATION OF A REGIME

Mankind has forever been persistent in the adoration of the use of slaves and the conviction of using these slaves for any means. To this we know however to end such slavery a consigned documents for approval to end it is forever overused by many powerful regime. It is noted that being "emancipated" in doctrines to the development of a system after the destruction of a regime capitalized on authoritative measures. The mind of the individual can never emancipate-it is seen notably in their action, in their proverse, reluctant, acceptance of the old way, the rebellious way, non-conformity of a new regime.

A METHOD ON SYSTEM OF CONTROLMENT

The 21 St century, a century as we know today belongs to the hands of the "idealists", that the ones that have the creative devilicious, destructive, liturgy of death, where no matter how powerful it may be, caught rival between human sacrifice and the system in existing power. But there is a method, one system can follow, welcome to an idea, so farvastly it can work. To this is called the:

DOOMDAGE

The doomdage is describe as a system within a system-however this system accommodates all creative idealists, who are not in conformity to the likes of the system but is rewarded with the full likes of a system. A "replica" of a system it's called. To those who accommodates this liking of the system do everything that every citizens does, to be an average individual. The system will no longer find any statue of a "dollar" to keep such individuals alive. And failure to acknowledge-starvation to their own cause it will be—To those non-conformists will share likes of being employed. But odd jobs will be within their framework of the existing system but for a minimum of working hours it shall be and back to the doomdage it shall be. Where a welcome met shall be awaiting them, guarded by the finest uniform officers of the system. Their workforce employment shall be paid and their needs and wants shall be rewarded within their "replicated" system, such order to survive.

Community information or societal strategic information networkls important to a democratic system-whereby such information on all citizens living in a community or society will make it easier for the system to operate its workforce.

SYSTEM CONTROLMENT 2

There can be many words to describe the behavioural pattern of citizens in a nation. Not every aspects a system may provide goes to the liking of every citizens or neither the systems economical growth are allowed to the liking of all citizens. When these attributes of behavioural uncontrolment occurs, new words are used to describe new behaviours.

Separatisms can be broken down into two:

{1}Non—conformists—where the citizens, individuals, societies perform no liking to the system in any way.

{2}Non-reformists-Where reformation is difficult to this goes both ways to an existing system workforce or either the citizens who are disillusioned

Separatists-Are citizens who perform no liking to systems and finds new demeanors to fuel their fiery wage, either funded by foreign aiders or the good will of the people.

Revolutionaries-Are citizens who fight for a change, worth fighting for regardless which entities differ in reasoning. To most other forms of movements, these battorialists are the regular citizens seen as nationalists to the system, but formalities better the uniform.

An "inhibitor"-Is someone who has the ability to introduce an idea to a sector, group or network of societies that may cause tension or absolved the matters at hand.

A foreign interventionists-Are individuals or either groups that are introduce to a system defaults and by understanding these defaults, enters such systems either by the governing leader or by the governing society{at war with the existing system} to further the causes and adhere to their claims. Sometimes the use of technology further their causes and to this neither are the inhibitors or their contributors are seen within the domain of the society.

NOTE: The dead can only wish for what they may have not done but to the living, can only wish that their life is spared enough, to live an understanding, to "live" the life of the dead. And it is important to "pray" and keep thoughts of the inevitable within our minds and honor it to our hearts content.

CHAPTER VII

UNIFORM POWERS

THE UNIFORM

There is a lot to talk about "a uniform" but a uniform has no "master" not even the system leaders, who appoints laws and regulations to govern its effectiveness, decisiveness and disciplines by allowing preferences to these preferred individuals who are chosen by ranks and seniority or otherwise bravery to govern, control the exuberance authority of a "uniform", hence the reason for having ranks.

So it is that "a uniform" has enough power alone to effectively institute enforcement of laws and regulations. The bearing of arms and anthems they follow, ensure their effectiveness at work.

But remember no matter how superior creative idealist creates their endeavours to allow a sovereign uniform to be all-powerful, the individual behind the uniform cannot be less of a "smirk" to be not powerful. So does an individual need to wear a uniform to be powerful? Or is it the way around?

Uniform has made their way throughout history by "individuals" who themselves have built within them an amour that is undefeatable.

And this armor allows the individual to create or recreate a uniform to their liking thus allowing the sovereignty to rise.

Any individual that is considered to be powerful and understand the uniform, who then creates a new uniform, this is what always happens and will always be.

UNIFORM APPAREL AND THE INDIVIDUAL

Uniform apparel and a uniform individual is two different strengths

{1} uniform apparel can take many shapes, colour and many emblems, stars and ranks. Uniform apparel always represents an existing system or organization. Uniform apparel can be recreated or newly created by any individual from a civilian government of authority or a member of a uniform organization.

Uniform apparel can be destroyed because it holds minimum of power. If a system is destroyed, so is the uniform because "a uniform is a representation of an existing system"

{2} a uniform individual—all human beings since the existence of mankind is considered a uniform being. Only "one" of us has ever been on this earth followed by "one" ideas so as such which makes us unique in our "one" ideas, "one" characteristics. A uniform individual.

{3} a individual who sees power within a uniform organization and not the uniform apparel or principles that governs it or the individuals presently representing it and has the power to create or re create a uniform apparel, constitute new governing laws of the uniform organization because such a individual sees the power of such organization as weak and powerless in it's effort is considered as a philosopher to the continuation of the word "uniform". Hence the reason why it is said that a "uniform" has no master because different intelligent minds would always come and go and yes! Would make an input but as times passes new superior minds would allow the uniform to be in existence and not allow it to be destroyed.

{1} the word "uniform"
{2} a uniform apparel
{3} a uniform individual
{4} a philosopher of the continuated existence of a uniform.

So the question is would a uniform empire always exist?

We can say that uniform and uniformity would always exists on this earth because uniformity is within every framework created by mankind.

But "uniform" essence and force has escaped from the framework of man's intelligent invention for years which dwells supernaturally amongst mankind.

Only those who posses' superior minds can see its force and harness its strength and when they do can bring it to their own creation. And when it does, you can witness that anytime individuals powerful enough to capture it; it is only for one purpose to join a uniform apparel and a uniform goal, that somehow makes history.

So can we say that the uniform force is for uniform individual thinkers who seek to create a uniform apparel, hence a uniform organization?

Sounds like biasness but there would always be certain force for certain power, that's why there is a separation because if these powers would come together to become a full force entity, disaster would occur, hence the statement "the uniform is a powerful entity by itself and when a superior minded individual knows about uniformity joins such powers together to become "whole".

Super superior such individuals would become. That is why a uniform individual must be superior in order to capture the uniform force and introduce it to a newly created uniform apparel organization.

Note: a uniform force once captured would not join a uniform appareled organization that is already there. It must be created from the pigmented mind of a uniform individual.

Note: the separated period is known as the kingship period where philosophical minds destroyed the king and queens lavish lifestyles thus interfering with the powers they had attained. The power to govern, the power to rule by law, the power of the uniform.

Throughout history many minds had created new powers to govern and to rule by law thus within every system government and justice stand alone and powerful while the "uniform" follows orders and is not used to harness its full strength.

Few individuals around the world have done it and bravo to them! In the ages of the king and queen, the uniform is what brought "status" to the king. The will to conquer lands to populate and expand their ruleship. It is expected that superior uniform individual who believes in the continuation of the uniform force would search and harness its force into their created entity or uniform apparel organization.

Foremost:

The uniform is a slave to the existing two powers because such entities within the system do not want such entity called the "uniform" to rise again.

The philosophy of having a man of embodied physically strong and skillful individual within the masses of the population of a nation as ever been the framework ideology for many. Seen in the ancient times, medieval times, post—modern era and the modern era to which we stand here today.

The "warrior" attitude for some human beings enhanced their thinking to acknowledge that a war could be any day and preparation is crucial, hence be always ready for engagement.

Thus it is their belief that the uniform or any knowledge that surrounds its existence cannot or never be similar in strength to the creative genius that efforted their work towards the continual existence to government, governance, ruleship and law also the ideological minds that have the justice system so unique and supreme.

Therefore any system that attempts to create a uniform system made out of their pigmented mind. Some system solely depends on the continual existence to their cause for ideology towards governing and the justice negates any attempts of having any within the systems of the world.

A uniform society at work, done in some aspectorial prophecy or some propaganda at large to enslave the uniform? But no matter the enslavement

The uniform has their place in the works of the inventive minds of man.

Warfare throughout history always "mutates" but their tactics by many combatants never change which consists of "military" training and military weaponry. So as such in this 21st century a mutated warfare is at our doorstep ready to enter our door and trampled our households hence the reason the uniform has to be effective because "would the politicians have the courage to control a combatants urge to purge society ills?"

We live in a combatant world, a will to be ready and engage fully to all works ahead and let danger be our last concern, initially. The suit and tie business only works well when the uniformed units take their pride away and pull forth their courage to defend an honors worth to a stable a stable system.

THE UNIFORM POWER

The uniform supersedes all types and foundational systems of power collectively and holistically. No power can ever be greater than a uniform power and a uniform individual who performs function relating to uniformity surpasses all divisional and individual power holders. This uniform power few only sees and few ever hold its power because its power holds the source to understanding "warfare" at a different level, "survival" at a supreme level and covertly opens all doors, relating to secrets to the expansion of the mind.

These traits are the secret endeavour to better the judgment of a human being in these times of solderists activities.

{1} UNIFORMITY—is the highest supreme forms a human being can posses. Any human being with strong unbreakable values which is embedded and becomes part of such being transcends a resounding renaissance throughout any system at work. Such practitioners of uniformity posse's wisdom beyond their age and always seek interest to change what is not there to what can be there.

Philosophers, idealists, inventors are just a few that find domain within governance, religion, sciences and self-appraisal issues of the mind, body, spirit.

{2} UNIFORMITY to a uniform apparel to a UNIFORM SYSTEM—these are individuals who uses their uniformity powers to greater the use to a uniform system at work. Such individuals here are somewhat different than a regular philosopher, proclaiming work of issues like adaptation to the mind and the use of it or finding greater force within to channel its energy towards your daily lives.

But just a few mention here. An individual who searches this part are considered the most "power" individuals within the world works. Due to the fact that, the uniform apparel, the uniform organization, the practice of uniformity are three separate power. One must have superior power to hold these three domains.

But there are different levels of uniformity an individual can achieve

{1} uniformity—a gift few attain but their growing stages depends on the discipline of such an individual.

{2} a supreme uniformity—a individual who posses strong mental conditions to face an ongoing opponent to a fiery war of the mind and their possessive capabilities.

These individuals here, the power to shift any created structure, created by many minds, recreated systems, create interventions or destroy inventions and their inventitive minds that created them.

Individuals who practice the uniformity gifts to a uniform organization are considered supreme uniformers and are very unbeatable at their tasks.

A UNIFORM ORGANIZATION PRACTISING THE ART OF UNIFORMITY

Uniformity means togetherness, one embodiedness, a single organization with "one" belief. Within a uniform organization all individuals weary such representative of the uniform apparel thus the uniform organization must be of "one" mind and body.

That is what makes uniformity, of a uniform organization so unique. So as such, no other entity other that a uniform organization cannot fulfill these attributions.

All individual bearing such uniformity must think alike, survive alike and be superior in their work alike, like no other. This is real practitioners of uniformity, this is how and why it is a greatest must to be beloved to this cause.

This cause, disallow any interference from outside civilian interventionists, when a power is strong within its "confines". Disenchantment can prove the entertainer of such action to cause some form of ripple effect of, which in turn then cause a effect which produces, bewilderment to formulate and control the uniformers are great, there no authority given power can separate its bond.

A bond is what must be attained within a system where human emotioners can trigger off a setback; results are and can be fatal to the uniform. The bond is not acknowledgement of persons and their traits but their great aspiring knowledge within their conceptualized minds.

WARFARE

Warfare—is a word that has a very exquisite inspirational ideology behind its existence. There are two main types of warfare, which depicts the understanding and the initial creation from the perspective of the human body—

{1} there is the warring ideology of the human mind, where the warfare type is of the mind and the creation of the continual existence of who combator posses the most powerful ideals and ideas.

{2} warring ideology of the physical body, where skills and physical strength rules the battlefield entirely.

{3} both in harmonic existence.

Warfare is just like a "virus" it mutates but no matter how much it mutates it is still "virus" and still carries its traits.

Warfare mutates but it still carries the traits of warfare, no matter how much effort and implication it carries or the change in design or location, it is still warfare.

And as usual the only "uniform" equipped to control any type of warfare tactics is the "military" uniform. Nothing else can match up to this mantra no matter how sophisticated within the city area where building structures are enclosed and masses of people are evolving to make means of employment, requires tactical units, which have the introduced knowledge of strategizing the outcome of success within this area.

Without the knowledge of strategizing, failure would be their triumphant moment.

Warfare within the city limits provides any soldiers with struggles to appoint positions especially if the opponents gain the upper hand or upper ground. Here skills of the mind and courage would lead the day of battle. Here the commander would have to create battlery laws for that position. A great leader can read hundreds of books on strategy position in any field of battle but remember a lot of philosophers and idealists are joining militant and rebellious groups so adhering to mutation in tactics.

No longer is military tactics ruling the day but philosophical military minds. So the commanding leader must know how to strategize and believe in their own style of creating a battlery law towards the battle at hand. This knowledge not only goes for the military but for all uniformers that bear arms.

During the ages of the early 1900's both uniform "the police and the military" showed common tactical and superior knowledge only both uniformed organization were unbeatable.

The police service was superior in controlling societal governance and the military superior in controlling the governance of the nation. After that period coming up to the mid 1800's, the mind of these individuals separated their superiorness and placed them in their own division. Hence the reason why terrorisms continues to destroy the framework of societal governance because the police service, lacks superiorness to control these tactical efforts made by combatants or opponents of the states existing system, hence the reason why "I" state that the "uniform" is a very powerful entity by itself and is the only entity that has been in existence since the existent of societies and population that choose to govern and institute a type of governance.

For survival of self and these recognized as friends to self as a part of uniformity organized. Thus when a commanding leader reads a lot of books and makes note that reading these books are to prepare you about the enhanced mutation over the years and to equip you about thinking a new way, than the way you were before.

It is not to use towards your new warfare in design. Warfare in the air, where superiority is readed because air support in any battle is important and this introduction lessens ground troop's fatalation. Any commanding leader must know ground troops is important in any war, due to the advances in war technology is important.

This 21st century, where every movie or strategy has been seen and sorted into books can no longer be effective. Hence the reason new warfare by these militant groups are targeting distressed nations to fuel their rage.

Warfare in an open field, armor is needed and support by air fleet minimizes causalities of ground troops "shade" or enclosed area is important in a strategizing war. Too much open field proves fatal to both combatants.

Shade warfare—shade warfare proves great to a strategist at arms. The ability for camouflagement is great no matter where the field of battles is located. If a combatant can "lure" their opponents into a particular "shade area" where tricks of battlery is introduced and ready a winning time, would be acknowledged. But if one opponent introduced such movement due to loss of troops or less artillery to minimize the loss and maximize the remaining as great "shade warfare", camouflages any opponents weakness even if their opponents knows such weakness.

Note—warfare in an area must be carefully looked at before engaging an open area of battlefield in fortunate for disasters if not purported correctly. A foreign engagement into a landmass where shade is high, the engaging soldier must use its degrees, if an area with high positionary wantingment an introduction of shade must be met by any means.

Shade—can also be inducted to city buildings where shade is high as well as position but entry to a high rise area where opponents have the upper hand cannot be met by no way by vehicular transportation by any war vehicles.

TYPES OF WARFARE

There are three types of descriptive warfare:

{1} creative type
{2} induced type
{3} individual type

Masters of all these three are considered to be magnates to every battle

{1} creative type—creativity to visualize, to adopt an idea, transforming these ideas to a philosophy, the philosophy is then further transformed to such individual creative autonomy to devise at all levels of work. The creativeness is then put to paper and when seen, paper and when seen, proper analyzing would be used.

If additional information has to be introduced, then the use of another means called "strategizing" is planned. The better such individuals creativity is, the better the outlook to plan is far greater.

An appointed place for war is just an area where mankind had no cause to develop it is just there. The nature's way of giving something to man but the mind, there in the "skull" can never be an appointed place of war because the mind can reach through depths, thus allowing such place for further development.

Think of the mind like a "city", this city engulfed with different people, different structures and different information available and see how people within that area can "govern" themselves without any interference from any domain.

{2} induced type of warfare—this type deals with the character of the individual after all creativity has expanded the mind to better operate. It's up to the individual to have enough courage to allow this creativity to surface within the mind of mankind.

If such actions are primitive more work needs to be done, if indeed great and explosions of emotions and anarchy are felt a great surprise "yes" but these actions would allow this individual to become stronger in such efforts until an opponent has arise to destroy all work ahead.

These are the real example for inducement, to see the power that lies within the idea and the creativity.

{3} individual type—individual who loves to battle can show signs of bewilderment. You can know not their actions now and then only if such individuals decide to let such information to be pronounced.

However individual type, where this topic of understanding is not like the others, where such individuals must be strong in their feats or must know battles and be a warring factor to any fighting cause. This deals particularly with a different type of warfare, the warfare of the individual mind. Camouflagement is the word here which must be induced to an individual with a particular trait. This trait of "discipline" and to be "silent" would, when practice can have a discipline outlook to life's struggle and created battlefields. Silent soldiers are what they are called. Their ability range from:

{1} strategizing without any ones attention
{2} planning a major battle but remains silent and resilient to its cause
{3} a powerful mind when such actions are seen but such individual remain discipline to the outlook until day of silent planning would put them down in definitely. A powerful mind is their greatest feats these silent soldiers posses. The will to kill without being seen or any traceable evidence to be found. In any warfare, their position would be a "strategists"

To find reason to an outcome position maybe losing or winning. You can also notice that even if winning such individuals never shows such congratulatory mood, for another readiness for another battle is soon approaching.

The battle equipped the battler, the ways to implore "silent shadowless soldiers". Are individuals who posses gifts to not be seen but their existence are there but can remember that being a "soldier" means one thing, the built to survive, put servility with shadowless—means that there is an advantage to their war and to be silent at its coming or inception.

Well! A perfect soldier I might add. Creation of new ways of a soldier can never be far fetching because no matter how important a system wants to survive throughout generations "the uniform" is the only entity that can fulfill that dream.

BATTLERY LAWS AND SURVIVAL LAWS

There are two amongst others that which described upon a system can be noticeably great and seen. There are many laws governing warfare for there are and where many philosophers and idealists who posses their own perspective on laws on survival.

But generations have seen that types and laws governing warfare in the perspective of a gifted superior individual who has captured the essence of the system uniform and its continual survival would possess a different perspective of warfare than a non bearer of a uniform. Look at two powerful laws that I have created, I an idealist for a uniform have described

{1} battlery laws
{2} survival laws

—note initially that there are systems that posses a good governance and bad as well, a system destroyed also known as a "red nation\ battorial nation" or a land mass occupied by a varied of intelligent people who have to decide on the now than the later, were every decision is crucial.

Battlery laws cannot exist within the domain of the laws of survival, when it has to do with specific aspect. So tender they rests on, that decisions must be wise if a combattorial sees as such to use such laws in a system.

Take note why such statement is said

[a] in a good governing system, where there is no anarchy no matter what the governing type are, there can never be no reason for the citizens who posses different influential powers to do battle unto their desired aspectorial functions because the system works for them.
[b] in a bad governing system where anarchy is present due to different faction creating their own philosophies other than

the foundational fathers rests upon, there will be means for citizens to create their own battlery functional laws against the opponents to determine the victor.

However survival laws would be introduced, so as such in order to create battlery engagement, one must know how to create laws to survive continuously until "a" goal is met. Here the system performs no liking to the citizens, a broken chain would suffice to acknowledge.

[c] red nations\ battorial nations—this is where a system of governing was in place, past tense but no longer there but the removal of this system was not met by a strong decisive "follow up".

System to replace it but instead due to chaotic behaviour of the citizens to repel to any new form of governing type has forced this nation to be recognized as an occupied landmass, filled with people who have no choice to recommend ways to survival and battle for that continual survival.

This is called "the will power of an embodied mass of people to destroy the framework of system to which was there without a proper management to institute a follow up system to replace its destruction—proper planning".

BATTLERY WARFARE

There are all types of warfare ever created. Let us take for instant these societal warfare\ gang warfare—this type of warfare is considered a favourite one in many countries and the only factorial opponents is the forces made to control its presence. And that is the police enforcement agencies.

If this force is not equipped properly in all measures, a doom of opportunity will come crashing down. These gangs operate within a society, where most of the citizens occupy there and still "loyal" to the system.

Thus making it harder to recognized these gangs, whether how viable and noticeable are there actions. It is not like such society for the system is just these individual have a knack for destruction and an urge for battle for territory to demand respect. For these warfare are no different to a nation fighting another for territory.

[b] small scale war—these conventional warfare, the shoot outs with combattorial individuals, no mass groupings, just only in small scale.

[c] large frontal war—this is where two territories are separated only be a border and such territories who resides close to such borders uses detrimental machines to destruct the other close by. This action can only force any opponent here if tiresome effort is seen. A frontal attack, it's the other side will be certainly attained.

[d] extraction warfare—where the main goal is to extract individual from a controlled area, where such controlled one would become hostile when engaged by any opponents. Major success can be, when extraction is needed one must never use "ground troops" only use means of "airlift"

[e] battlorial battlers—where any nation can become a battlefield if ever engaged by any opponent or can be called "battorial nations".

Note—that ground troops are very essential in ensuing a war is soon if there can be no more soldiers to fight, then who will man the machines and to this acknowledgement any general is order to use ground troops in any type of warfare, must introduce "cover camouflagement" so such ground troops can camouflage in these cover or any man made covers.

BATTLERY LAWS FOR TRAITORS TO A UNIFORM

{1} All bearance of the uniform must be stripped off in front of a parade of uniform in column and must be burn alongside with the individuals profile and records must be nill and void for any eyeing individual

{2} the individual must make a statement before such shall meet their doom.

{3} the individual then would be able to perform duties that are very disliking. This attacks the individual well being to react in a certain space of mind.

{4} experimenting with various theses allows the individual to become subjects to the cause.

A DECREE

When an ator make a declarative decree of order to wage war unto a separatist society at work—this act is regarded as the beginning of creative ideas of warfare that must be induced once created. This decree goes by superior order 1st—the declaration to create new commanding laws that would govern the existing battlery laws.

2nd—the declaration to create new commanding laws that would govern the existing survival laws.

3rd—the declaration to create new commandment to rivalries.

THE BATTLERY LAWS OF COMBAT MODE OF AWARENESS

It's human nature that every individual would eventually have to declare battle unto another for all or few different reasons. However not all posses human attributes. Some posse's gifts, extraordinary gifts that supersedes all other potential gifts.

{1} an ator must always acknowledge battles are important no matter what form proceeds itself

{2} an ator must know that the way you are personally many will try to figure your uniqueness and superior qualities. This attitudes begets into warring individuals

{3} an ator must be aware of individual who conversate with you, for all may not posses gifts and like humans that we are uncontrolled emotions do exists and envy, jealously do occur.

{4} an ator must be aware that letting others know your gifts is sometimes overused for favouritisms can be the benefactorial means here to become somebody but not everybody would accept your words and the meaning it portrays.

{5} an ator must stand their grounds and be very strong minded to their own beliefs in uniformity and what area of expertise they should follow.

{6} an ator must be aware of their peers and always engage in battle mode. Battle mode comes in many ways by the use of survival tactics, interluding tactics, attack tactics, which means formulating a plan of action.

{7} an ator must always pre plan a mock trial of any situation that can plan an attacking force which can generate multitudes of disasters. For many mini battles can escalate to a disaster, if not controlled or become overexposed to other elements which surrounds contagious ideas.

{8} an ator life is "discipline" that's the motto—for an ator does everything which follows discipline. An ator objective is to create laws to govern a battle and the survival laws which allow any ator to only survive during the enactment of the battlery laws and rivalry laws.

{9} an ator must know that every individual cannot understand the limits to an atorian ideology. Hence the reason an ator must know that emotions can run high if not controlled by controlling all emotion. Then an ator can fully be engaged to onslaughtment

{10} an ator must always focus, it comes times when a lot of negative forces surround your mind and instances where no friends or companion stand to your side. An ator must understand here, when you a soldier practices "uniformity" and hence "singular supreme uniformity"—is knowing the fact that you are supreme and to allow your creativity to be powerful, one must not ask for help, let your own uniformed ideas work for you.

Then and only then shall you become indestructible and your combattors shall really show their face.

{11} an ator must be aware that compassion destroys the capability of any true soldiers and to acknowledge that it comes a time when an ator must know that destroying opponents can be the best way for security within a sector.

Note: a battle field can be any place, any time appointed. Two or many gathered at a point not appointed or created by any opponents can be described as a on spot battleground. This on spot battleground surrounds the concept of "survival laws" where the opponents would have to use their skills within to master that on spot battleryground.

When an opponent decides to escapes an on spot battleryground where such opponent feels insecure, then the opponent, if knows such area can then find a nearby positionary location more fitting for the opponent.

This can be called an appointed positionary battleground. This follows battlery laws, where you have to create new laws for the battle. Hence the reason why in every battle one must create their own new laws in relation to the condition, than to mesmerize a note from a book. This can allow the brain to become fixated in other dilemmas and not focus with the tasks at hand.

AFFIRMATION TO A UNIFORM POWER

The uniform entity would remain supremely powerful over all other adversarial powers combined or of singular strength. The uniform powers conquers all power, destroys all weather; deserts storms and official in suites. The uniform power condemns all atrocities of any kind against any individual "ranks" in order.

For those who try endlessly to conquer them who reside on these powers shall enter into a hostility war with or without preparedness.

The uniform powers of individuals who assimilate growth in their personal reach, begets their cowardness, attitudal, force and attempts to conquer "a" uniform power by choice. Supremely powerful one shall be, therefore the introduction of "adversarial powers" are to be enacted.

1ST ORDER TO ADVERSARIAL POWERS:

{1} adversaries are a must—it incorporates the mind to better understand your judgement rather your combatants.

{2} adversary must be tamed and controlled when their weakness are found. This weakness shall be used to your advantage in either information wise or personal up growth.

{3} adversary must be looked upon cautiously and must have a "history" to which you must know. To all survivalists have their individual traits or markings they leave at a battle end.

{4} adversary are humans beings similar to you combatant, therefore since you cannot interpret their judgement, henceforth, you do it for them, by putting anger within the movement, thus looking forward for an reaction if either this should allow you to understand your opponents mind of state\ readiness

{5} adversary can only be skilled if the first strike is their deadly, so no wastage of force can be seen.

{6} adversary carries "force", some may be evil or good. Be warned about this human you are but if spiritual reckonings do posses your will to fight, then let out your burst of action.

{7} each fight "wins" increases your adversarial powers. This is how humans' battlefields are met. Hence the reason each warrior has a "history" compiled about their behaviour in a battlefield. The more you win, the more power is gain physically, mentally and sociably within your "honored men"

{8} adversaries can approach you at any given time. It is a must that all combatant should create "laws" of survival, survival made in all created development, tactics in a given situation.

This is would develop the mind into a fighting apprentice towards your aggressor or pacified combatants.

{9} adversarial powers can be given without over fighting for such the will to apprehend a battle and make a decision that you are supreme and you must "forfeit" it. Knowledge is important then so shall it be.

ADVERSARIAL RIGHTS

{1} if a combatant and or such implementation of an army shall forfeit a battle, one must put in writing reasons for forfeiting and with drawing and as such, the leader shall forthright all assets that produce income and growth.

The rest to substance a minority shall be given to them so as such to use some intelligent ways to evolve such.

{2} a forfeiter shall forfeit their life to the winning opponents so as such shall not be "killed" or permanently scarred but must be kept alive until such is no longer needed.

{3} adversaries have the rights to delay a battle or war, so as such must put in writing, reasons for delayedment, within one day and provide some military supportive arm as collateral.

{4} adversaries have rights to proclaim propaganda to their nation or others but must live up to that reputation either new or the latter wars.

{5} adversaries have the rights on a battlefield as mentioned. If battle readiness is not up to mark but still decides to go ahead regardless of their improprieties, one shall be acknowledged to understand same and it's "honor code" and "character code" in a battlefield appointed.

One must allow same to provide a good battle but battles is no joke! Prepared or not must fall to their direly cause and the others chosen to survive must perform penance duties to the winning combators by means of hard labour.

{6} adversaries have the rights to proper burials on lands appointed as heavens gateway to all soldiers of battle, for they fought for and what they fought for must die neither their ideology which stood out at that "era" of work.

{7} adversaries have the rights to be properly equipped, properly trained; properly perform the art of fighting beautifully, properly remembered for a lifetime.

Note: adversarial powers and rights are for the uniform powers and not any other entity. For these soldiers in uniform are the guardian of the states and the keepers of their souls from other men ideology and philosophy to greater judgemental creations.

ACHIEVAL LAWS

To dominate or to achieve a goal, that can be responsible for a developed situation this benefits any soldier of legit command

{2} battles are great feats to enjoy, however there comes many different battles and many different opponents towards these battles, creating new battlefields where a soldier stands

{3} laws are created to discipline the mind, achieval laws are no different. Writing commandmental laws to govern an "action" towards a detached reaction allows a submental being a sense of becoming closer to a understanding of achievability.

{4} as a human trait, achieving efforts within the views of those who possess no gifts or talents are watchers towards your development and as a soldier must always be committed towards an action, a goal, a routine of governance. Never deter from it.

{5} an achieval situation brings forth action of those who encircles you daily, a sense of wantedness and a sense of friendship. For this is just a mimic reaction towards your success, be firm and opposed towards these newly emotional friends

{6} an atorian has no friends, wants no companion of friends. For they stand alone. Soldier if you consider yourself to be an "ator" a true combattor you must adopt regulations rules and commandment that governs your actions alone. Any new information, be speculative about it.

{7} achieving is a norm to us human beings but to achieve a soldiers dream is different from any dreams. To want power and to govern its attributes, only few are assets to such power.
Within any organization find yourself worthy to such system and create "new orderation" which govern s a new action that will force these existing laws to be abolished

{8} only few soldiers are able to create new laws. Consider yourself lucky and extraordinary to create and to destroy those created by men of stature, well powerful you are.

{9} achieval laws are only for soldier and their continual performation to their success not for the faint hearted and non soldiers to a regime.

ENEMY AND ARCH ENEMY

In warring faction there is a word frequently used in warfare, this word prescribed as "enemy". To I the true combattorian "an enemy" is a powerless word that us soldier use to demise an attention only fitting to our cause.

Hence if you, a combattor standing on the northern bank creates an ideology that few adopts and the rests decide to leave the province and enter the southern bank and create a new ideology, you the northern who need land to occupy territories to expand your ideology decides the southern province must join or die. Thus introducing the word "enemy" and due to the introduction of this the southern decides you attacking them for no reason then calls you their "enemy" to their cause.

This has shown that solderrisms in the battlefield of the physical ideological aspects is a favourite amongst the dynasty of sectorials.

POLITICAL MISCONCEPTION AND THE UNIFORM CONCEPTS

It is known that the political struggles of the independent minds of philosophers before time immemorial have created great ideas to govern mediated masses. However due to the evolution of minds during the years and the mutation of ideas have somehow brought the concept that "can political science reign supreme always?".

The uniform, which is controlled by the ideology of politicians, over the years have made bad judgement on situations due to their unmannered approach to solutions and problem fixing, that reached a stage where the uniform, which follows orders without questions become enforcers to individuals principalities and destruction to their own finite power to make decision on their own.

Death and destruction had caused many known wars and battles to be recorded in history due to the untrained, unprofessionalism and weak survivalists' temperament of politicians.

This, the 21st century, where a new enemy has approached the will to create ideas of terror and masses of the populist's convulging to create hysteria. Note that these politicians adopt a "know it all" approach, where they send the uniform to participate this continual behaved approach.

If some die, depending on honor which is corrupt you die for freedom, you die for democracy or any other continual independent system

Note that warfare is meant for one uniform and that is as such—a regiment body of officers in uniform made to survive superior fitness and strategy skills of adaptation to be supreme, which is as such the army, battalions to name just two.

A, politician knows nothing completely about warfare or the advancement of its entity. The uniform is the only entity made fittingly to control warfare, the uniform along a continual initiative with advance chaotic behaviour must be allow to used their uniform powers to annihilate all mischievous individualists or societies.

Hence, the political science misconception differs with a uniformer concept. Leave the war for the uniformers, the professionals! It takes courage for who create these proclamations of war and do not be there where battlery is concern and gets to live another day, while the uniformers and their practice to it, die fighting for a cause not concernly met by any politicians—call them "heroes to cowardice acts"

Their coward's principle rules:

{1} to hide behind the uniformers, I a politician, a great debater makes mass approach with insensible thinking and allow my great army to follow my actions. I am powerful here.

{2} to make many friends even enemy masses of the state; I control and give lavish gifts to avoid targeting my people and hurting my tenure as leader.

{3} sacrifice soldiers' lives, to allow anarchists to overtake a country to my benefit.

{4} sacrifice my troop's life to benefit on wealth and a fame to my name that can cause unjust life to others.

{5} create a tension between two nations so as to allow I to intervene and introduce my wrath of beastly features and cause a uproar and a war to get a name and a fame to carry out throughout history.

A HEROES PRINCIPAL RULES

{1} to take in charge, in all situations, no matter the danger, let the skills acquired be your guide and your senses.

{2} to know your boundaries and your weakness in every given attempt. Avoid crowds or stunts that can be detrimental to your life. "Think taught before a untaught action is to be given"

{3} know danger of hand and know where to go. To many soldiers and untrained individuals who gives names to themselves without no assertive force. Before you damage any untrained individuals and call yourself into attention, avoid it.

{4} all heroes are great warriors but it is good to not show any skills to get fame. The silent you are, the better you blend into an environment.

{5} an appointed job can produce a hero, one that outshines all others within a profession, go by a unique decree. All heroes posses their own decree, which some follows and those who forgets these principles and end up in an unfavourable position.

{6} heroes comes and goes, bravery always choose those who neglects the word "madness" from existence and adopts a curious entity within their minds. Develop this and you shall see this come true.

{7} a hero goes by many aliases, triumphant soldiers ready to get in aim and shoot the target at its heart. A position where they know they can never get a helping aid. A hero must know this—the one strike fatality hit which can permanently put any combatant down.

{8} a hero is someone who uses their talents for any means and how it is shown depends on the ability of the helpless who need such help to accept it as true heroism.

Many are chosen to wear a uniform and represent its power in battle or in engagement but few would be chosen to fight alongside its power.

THE WISHING OF ME

There is nothing to wish upon me or either do I shall use my optimum power to wish, for I neither need such an adoration. For wishing are for those who yes! Consider themselves searching of a betterment in life's worthwhileness but "I" who is considered a "wish" for someone had during a time of neglect did wish upon the stars for an entity like me, so close was the choosing of this entity that I became a "growth" with a spectrum of imagination and due the laying of the imagination the wish was given more strength to its caliber.

Thus "I" was beginning to grow until I was fully emancipated and brought forth from an imagination to a sketch of paper to the real of the helm that non idealist considered the dark ages in the 21st century.

For "I" would be the only supreme being to bring back what is rightfully belong to the real soldiers here on earth. The right to live! For such a being who wished for this existence of being, to be inherited in this world and to be named a warrior of all warriors would soon be a legend to be made.

FINAL AFFIRMATION

I AM IN NO WAY DIFFERENT TOO ANYBODY IN MIND—BODY-SPIRIT, I CAN SEE WHAT YOU SEE-BUT MY INQUISITE MIND, CANNOT COMPREHEND IN THAT WAY-MY MIND THEN BECOMES A DOORWAY, TO BECOME INTRUSIVE TO ADD FURTHER INFORMATION TO SUCH DEVELOPMENT-THUS MAKING ME TO UNDERSTAND A DIFFERENT WAY OF THINKING-NOT SUBJECTIVELY BUT OBJECTIVELY, UNDERSTANDING OF THIS-ALLOWS THE MIND TO DEVELOP A NEW TASK OF DISCOVERING WHAT THE MIND CAN DO-—TO MUCH

SIMPLE THINKING CAN ALLOW ANY BEING TO BE SHORTCUTTED BY "CREATIVE IDEALISTS".

FINAL NOTE

Cartels—is an organization that thrives on the weakness of the mind, to those who want easy life, easy cash and wants nothing to do with the system.

FINAL SAYING

Sometimes your dreams is not what you perceive it To be-sometimes you are the "dream"-just showing Your presence-just showing the way how a dream Is to be-allows persons to have a dream

UNIFORMITY-SUPERIORITY-IDEOLOGY.

PART II

A WARRIOR'S HEART AND BELIEFS

A theory

A

Possibility that can exist

Readers note: a confirmation:

The reader on recongnising part II
Of this book, shall carry the name
"Ator"-a word dervied from the word
"comb/ator"

Ator is a champion name, for only a
Warrior can read this knowledge that
Will be bestowed, it is also a name to
Those who are willing to learn

CHAPTER VIII

The art to conquer.

SCROLL {1}

Oh!!!!! How I dream to conquer, long to drink blood of my enemies cup.

Here I am showing you the reader that I am going to describe as an "ATORIAN d COMBATORIAN".

Now you "ator" my friend, my colleague, my soldier at arms. You are about to witness first hands my testimony propheting in the art of conqueringment.

Understand it and understand it well, for I will leave a space for you to sign on the dotted line for our new contract at arms__________

_______________________________.

Failing to do this repercussion would be made to you.

Testimony prophesy day of this art begins: there is no turning back:

As I begin to endure unto another level, reminder of the satisfaction being-fought as a super being-taught as a super being, this superiority was called to an oath. For this I propose a silent moment that this volume of charismatic intelligence is bestowed as the "brain base" and this scrolled of beholders would be a finder of truthful knowledge—knowledge far understandable by the normal intellect, knowledge called

-governmental systematically ingrowned knowledge, that are slaved by their weak format of learning.

SCROLL{2}

My almost satisfaction: a point I took homily and self-righteously

I can never promise that I would never triumphantly rise to depths by your own stupidity but my continuation for more power would not be asked by God but be pulled forcibly by the "depths of elimination"—the dead zone darkness of the unreachable part of the brain. For I would make it a blessed "must" that world war three would begin at the tip of the destruction of the "sultans" "desert warriors" and their direly causes.

Once improvements lacks entirely—signs of new developments would take its place.

The important cause of this scroll is to improve the status of true "soldierism" to supremacy format by means of the:

-Dark commandments and the evilious rules governing this atrocity.

-Apocalytic anthems would be given as a choice of knowledge to be displayed against all forms of governments from the beginning of history of the world.

Take note that this would be the first and the last: justly noted, rightly owned.

SCROLL{3}

A calendrical inspiration brought upon me about time and how time is a factor towards conqueringment.

Let us begin: Time is an elemental—fundamental grouping for known successes. Elaborations on calculation on extreme measurements would tell the inspirator that limitation for growth inactment. It must be stabilized under tremendous horrors of advocations, vocally with time as a generation tool of worthy opponent for combating your determination against your actual doings. The less time you take solving improvements, great challenges would be fought instantaneously.

Groupings can be both wise and doctrinally, make means to solve massive calibrium problems to improve status control in the near future, causing successes at our young age.

SCROLL{4}

Here reader you will witness my observations and my emotions towards these observations

Laws are: But the only law described as the "military law". The military law on one particular calendrical time would be the benefactorial successor of all laws, the betrayal laws. However notes are polished to last for centuries-the pen "unique" in the stylish forms of expressions, disguised in the artry for:

Blockade anarchy: To the imaginable of the worse-grossly pocketing idea!

To the imagination to be corrosive multitude offspring's idea!

But the idea to have no idea without the use of idea-is the enactment of a sixth sense. This sixth sense, uncommon to be found, to at the ultimate end, results are miraculously to a scale of devastation.

As warriors knows it, consumption to the greatest, to the equality mechanizes onto competitiveness, whether if the opportunity comes and neglects a jubilation "kill or be killed" a concept for ridiculous attention. In the eyes of a hatred being comes closer to a belief of a soldier spirit.

The warrior one cast to damage, after finding what it takes to destroy without planning or consequences. This mind is certainly unplanned.

Observations on this "one" : The universal one requires the procedures of learning through the years and a process comes equally hazard when systems thought are system collaborated. Which in turn evolves the concept that educators of the past brought forth ideas of "governance" the way of "controlment" of the-at times-, misbehavioural minds to all types of government. History will also show the fail attempt of prolonged governing systems and noticing their havocation, other esteemed systems are rationalized but further inducement causes more un evolvement from these young educators. Effects are displacements and outcastments and rebellionists, which begins locally to a further-globally. To a disease of evilous motives and the destruction of what we know as the evolvement of the "brain". Combators who are you my friend would be subjective to an order to destroy all free brains and cast them to the pit of agonative condemnation as describe in the first edition.

Observation: To simple hate.

The simple hate people portrays becomes noticed by powerful beings called soldiers and seeing this, it evolves more powerfully. The resemblances are of their own but a revolutionary mutates all power which becomes a personality, causes lives to be lost. For times that are ahead incinerates the flowdarity of good. When comes simple tasking, devours temptations of reputable followers. So ator, our bodies were built to control and destroy the ideal concept of any person's thoughted mind to involve their intelligent mind for entrapment. Destroying their traps, destroys their self being-brain becomes brainless. Many occurrences come but cannot understand what is being seen.

Another observation as you will learn is "flagerism"-if you ator has witness my first edition you will know a different theory to this secret approach.

Let us begin: A five subjective fingers approach against an all ten oblivious ones comes a great test but a defeated ten trying best, yes!!!! Pitiful.

Flagerism—Is the ability of an educator to repudiate ideas of horrors onto patriots of nations including nationalities—or—to change corrupted views of a government by means of supreme intelligence and equipping this knowledge unto the nationals. Adhering this, give the patriots a bitter taste of their government falling by hands of misinterpreted, misleading ideas, thoughted to be "freedom of expression".

An act constituted by all democratic government an easy access to lurement. This form of knowledge comes in any "camouflage" design of speeches to the public. A large gathering format. Flagerism can also come as a single knowledge requiring no diction, just a format of "self sucking absorbant words" and showing courage to back up these words of fight.

Flagerism upon the people, if successful will prohibit the needs to conjure their diversities of civil laws known as judiciary, would be lowered to a detterent, second best rated motion to that of "military laws" governing both—provincial laws, state laws. Which in turn, the abominator seeks vengeance to trial military injustice, acts done by men of uniforms in battorial conflicting nations.

Now ator witness the Truesome Enduresome: Truesome enduresome is a singular meaning word of will minded power to challenge opponents as well as their counterparts to limits of expectations, guaranteeing that if ever to return as a citizenry you must forbid any prior knowledge of soldierism and pledge allegiance to the truesome citizens.

Order of command is silence, for the clouded mind of arrogance comes nonethingless than to a slow victory to a disappointed faction. Built to uphold any mishaps of occurrences to an untimely death.

SCROLL {5}

You ator are about to witness a form of anarchy prophesizing this power in the form of songs, this brings about more emmense power when songed upon the enemies of your expediency.

General-Auuluumedment-of-Magnitudment-Energies-{GAME}

Game—Towards higher form of thinking from a soldier in arms.

Auuluumedment—Is a affirmated supreme form of commandment. Not used by persons of regimed religious acts or governmental institutions. Auuluum commands comes under the most unadvised impossible tasks of commands. Auuluum actually requires age difference to knowledge difference. If any coherent coincident of survival methods to be actually formed in the "game".

Game—requires an edge of open-minded, fast intelligent thinking and of competitiveness, boldness. An engagement of noting, every events and events that are not enquirarable.

The 88th golden commandment rule—which is to be written as knowledge of monstrous correct living of a true soldier. Noted as a supreme form of command, still do not overstep the "dark commands" which is written under the "apocalyptic anthems".

ANTHEMS—Are a form of stylish writing which brings about to the reader a beauty of feeling for regulative distributions, due to its effect of its command style format.

You my "atorian" are about to witness some war anthems of conquerable efforts of destruction of the worldly events of present desires or "futureated" profits.

Oh!!!! How I dreamnt to sing these songs to drown my opponents throats with cutthroats lyrics and which i did.

{1} Longing for war.

Before I begin, there are three different types of war, my veteran soldiers, belligerent battles, dictating a war, mind games-a feudal war. What am about to sing to you, what war is really about, not what you have heard, not what you've seen

Hear me now!!!!!!-on my chosen form of war today is one of {fully—engaged—automatic—renewedment} in other words, I give you an anthem, my anthem, a soldiers anthem. To FEAR.

Chorus:

Longing we right on, we right on, we right on-we load-reload

Longing we right on, we right on, we right on-we draw-that cold of a gun

We make them eat boredom, triumphant we slaught them-show them whose boss, whose boss,

Determine to deter them, as we swerve to control them-shall emerse-the true first.

It all started with love but mounted to nothing, whats mines got to be yours, whats yours got to mines, it all counts down to a new mourning

Tricks of a new weapon, much better than your peace and your handy matrons

We ain't come here for the late night dinners, speeches about boring fake warriors

Which they say they spoke like cold hearted killers and your beastly wife at your side

What we are longing to do is kill and kill everyone in your chambers of fourteen rooms

To take over your people, yourself sucking people-the disgust we all feel it

Would wipe you out we can all see it

Murder is nothing compared to the 1st, 2nd, 3rd, 4th thousands we fought,

Held the world by a bloody cloth-mind those small unplanned wars, dictating

Some years of invading your worthless country—a country where your leaders keep hanging themselves and your people keep asking for help,

The small armed wars and the running and hide wars—you can't find that scripted in my art of war,

Lose your bloody fate-what-in-holy-name could do such a hatred in highly fate

Please God—please God give your sons blood as a shed, let me survive when the rain drops, drops red, am only human but god send.

End of song followed by the chorus.

{2} War is power, power is war:

This second item, is a favourite one:

Chorus:

Songs of joy, songs for the pain-songs for a soldier-ready in reign

War is power—power is war-bones with shield-tending no one

Songs for the living-songs for the dead-runs not your blood from the dirted ground-war is power, power is extreme-let's own this territory, let's make means to invade-trials of triumph it gains all respect

Songs of war-songs hellish is power—and {I} 2x

War {i}—is—power {i}—war is power—power is war

Songs of joy-songs for a ploy—songs of redeemers, sunged by underground threats

And—{I} 2x

My ator friend this is defined as classic chorus for the marching men in uniform to engage in battlery against the un battorialists.

{3}-Head under water means something for the fistful of war

War of my fist challenges everyday

War of my fist build corpse and catacombs,

Arise my benefit-conscript-obliverance guerilla.

Mighty, a mighty curses to own faults and redrawn

War of my fists don't cry on playing, war of my fist is shame of, game of.

-Ha!!!!!!!!! My atorian, another great chorus to sing onto-

{4} This particular item my ator, is one of my personal best. It reflects a lot of myself-the discipline life that from birth I still adore.

Greatest disgrate-grown up was straight

M double ii's—non stays alive, we wage raw war—it calls for close calls

What stays alive, what stays alive

Or I'll run your life-I'll run your life, bring me a trade and I'll free the slaves

Or you'll be on knees begging me please-till the under makes me free—this deal can be talked about to be agreed{I'll spare all lives} 3x

-Treacherous isn't it!!!!!!

{5} {the 8th guerilla warfare}: chorus—sunged 8x

Treacherous{3x} grunt—perfumed occasions you dying so blunt

Bigots-seculsists-that evil insults, left your soldiers stranded to rot

Pray for the informers to bring back good news, happiest moments brings tears-endless faction clues, what more can be stored-in this humanizing four for a foe-here am all bored all alone, snake do devours-my mouth bitter to a sour, stuffed in these rooms-am more of a do the assignations

Having won rivalries-make notice for the others

Come at me once again-cruel evil wraughts will pull at all restounders chorus

Am the only supreme being-resists no temptations

Conjections no reprisals-bias imitators-copycats infringe—stay focus-not focus

Concocted a story-the world would soon know it's a phony

Who knows? You knows?-it's an act putted out forth-we want to see him come out-want to see if he's real

Boa constrictors-prey out as predators

We swoop-choop—choop

Galoop-chuck who—{ch-oop—ch-oop}

Snuck who-betrayals at the backdrafts

Boobs don't go BOOM!!!

It ratta-ta-ta that fear, swear I swear, we can care, can care

8 can be identified as an eight team commandos—priviledge to no success, give reason to failure

8 is a name of a bomb—that 8 guerilla warfare—themed for many but one—you start run and you run, till that becomes overdone.

Ha!!!!!!!!! What treacherous music-this music my atorian is good for the soul, learn it for it is your task ahead to swell the head with over confidence before you enter a battle, these songs teaches you to forget the mistakes and eases your wounds.

SCROLL{6}

The rules of reigns: states that the conquered shall in every right make propositions to give their fighting cause a second domain. If unsuccessful, claimers of nations would be bestowed to inact laws of military in process. By the book, a brain base manipulated at its present form would take active to perform the duty of being the "beholder of dictated agumentated military laws". Their solutions should be "final". This system is not for the faint hearted, it arises from the mind of a supreme intelligent being who believes in the process of a military form of governing.

Rules of "sectorialisms"-noted that government's comes at all forms, not forgetting the "systems" governing these portfolios of true "governance". Sectorialisation comes immensely powerful—especially when its identity is unknowed. Secretcy is vagued.

What we are about to witness now atorian is what is noted shortly in my first edition the MAOC:

MILITARY AFFIRMATED ON OCCUPANTS DESIRES OF CHAOTIC-CY

Ha!!!!!!!!!! Ha!!!!!!!!!!! We have reached my favourite part of this art, showing you soldier that military governance is not farfetched and I will show you how.

Bitter arguments are that this type of forms is unknown. True to the fact that it's existence is having a lot of doubts.

-noted that the flag of bearance must be attained after being favourable to the war

-noted that the shield of authority, over the conquered state must be attained and stated after being rewarded to the war.

-noted that the music or the "words of fear" must be played in remembrance of your victory and the triumphant years of successes over the "periods of ideas"

-noted that the rules or the 88th commandments must be acted as a condition of over rulement and in condition that military presence must be assertive over the present.

Can a taken vocabulary word from a dictionary, which is written by scholars of some, which is, of a high esteemed environment to the English understanding. To better understand the ways to govern, can there be the use of the words "curiosity never becomes a necessity".

-the informinable causes it to be possible

-the dialect can be, the adjacent but the actions may be the point to "oppositeness"-cluelessness-obscurity. Discerning factions to belief by forwarding to the rule—MAOC. The art of "retrieval"

The governance: Governing purpose is and only would be that the individual transparent behaviour should remain outdoored and silent, till that day of action. Is noted and copied into major ideas, secondly performed into sketches to finally the day of TEST.

THE TEST TO CONQUEST

{Total—Eminism of an End to Secretcy-To Masterfully}

To then the quest begins, slowly but surely. The day of arrival on earth-counted as a number to build the birth status quo of the nation. Grown older and the traditional slain values are forgotten. Now comes a new technology of information added to a new form of vocabulary. Welcome to the "test of conquest".

The military system we shall call is "dettcoordians"—which is the introduction of laws, in relation to those who bears a uniform to the service of their country, creating one in favour to the uniform.

Take note reader this can never be accomplished by your finite brain—it is a prophesy meant for an existent existence, growing in proportion, so don't bother to try. Watch and observe this beautiful piece of brain at work, so one day you can understand that every force happens for a reason

88 Commandments

Or

Ages of soldierism rule

1st-military affirmated on occupants desires of chaotic-cy

2nd-bearance of arms

3rd-art of retrieval

4th-the governance

5th-test-d beginning

6th-test to conquest

7th-bearance of casualties

8th-controlment of the defeaters

9th-inactment of the laws

10th-changes of the laws

11th-destroying all constitutional acts of governments

12th-initalizing the coated shield of a new law

13th-the dettcoordian government is opened

14th-the books written on success of the dettcoordian laws must be opened

15th-the undefeated must prepare for war of conquest

16th-upholdment to information on "citizenry lifestyle" would be performed and constituted

17th-conquered nations must be on "notes of holdment". To adhere after defeated, must make readily actions successfully and justly

18th-no appointed leader must formally look to debates from the "red nations"-

{Nations that have been taken over by force, thus resulting in a bloody affair also known as red nations} or look to consultations from the "brain base network"—is a network similar to a war room. Start alone and measure your leadership lifestyle

19th-conformities of all success should be written, detailing the hands down access of powers from the red nations and deceits encouraged by less competitors

20th-re training and security would be a first guarantee plan and that no authority must be handed down to the former security agencies but our own

21st-soldierists anthems of dettcoordialism would be played and sunged by the interstated base soldiers and networked over the world

22nd-revival of the past governments would be accessible by notes and comparities of any disclosed similarities would be noted. For the judiciary systems would be under the law for civilians let alone the military laws would be the system to protection and governance of any men in arms in attempt to destroy a symbolic system of dettcordian or if a possible any ruling nations, which comes under the military act.

{1}-solderists arrests

{2}-conspiratorial arrests

{3}-flagerisms arrests

23rd-the day of wonment should be looked as the day of remembrance and should be noted

24th-sectorilisation of a particular race{classified} until attempts are made. For all defeated nations

25th-classification codes for each sectors of diversities would be opted to differentiate the unwanted

26th-these codes of sectors would be put to the test to rebuild the "red nations" and make it a defense zone. Until threats are made unlkikely

27th-no men in arms should look to refuge on these combated nations. For these nations are made only for defensive purpose

28th-if periods of tens are passed and looked as remembrance, then military presence of new governance would take its place to the new helm

29th-choose a great nation to achieve dormant activities with triumphant out goals and to keep to our own-if all fails likely nation of birth

30th-note: to rebuild or reconfigure a new army in due respect of not being an abominator to the soldierists cause. {1}Think {2} act {3}to defend. To two guards of strength, {1}the mind {2}the heart

These are the 30 rules-30 commandments of governing a nation and changing the aspects rigorously. For attempts to govern a nation to soldierists can be both a world war or interstate battlery or a, fascists coup-e-tat.

Now witness the commandments of living a soldierists way in the system of man

31st-pray at sun up and sun down, is inevitable to the great god. Prays should be a design of your own

32nd-gifts for power noticed at a young age must be given a opportune chance for resurrecting this gift of power, by controlling the wanton wastage of hands on intelligence

33rd-never confuse the idea of ever causing a collision of both factors of life

[soldierism and religion]—for these factors shows differences in battle

34th-the right to expand the brain-must be with compliance with the indepth growth of this desired gift

35th-the right to train for survival in defense and in skills is a attribute for soldierism

36th-commencement of survival must be no more than "periods of two"

37th-the right to learn the affairs of the past and present [governments\men of

Wars]

38th-the art of camouflage is practical-to give underminded analysis to the combattors who, willingly convert their cowardness

39th-the right of writing books of oversightment of the world over any generation upon at any present situation given

40th-the right to acknowledge the "day of decisions" would take its place. To decide which "fields" of interests is desirable until the "day of quest"

41st-the right to read the historians views on past inflictments and analyze strategies these "ators" took to defeat the combattors

42nd-the right of "inventing" a grand illusions of pictures to counteract the suggestions that are respected numerous of times

43rd-the command to enter the zone of elimination to depth of controlling feelings or emotions in times of distress

44th-the right to position yourself as an "ator" when time is approaching

45th-the right to yield enormous amount of physical power

46th-the right to not condone the feelings of love and friendship desires likewise the abominators

47th-the right to choose your successors by birth your chosen child

48th-the right to exercise the use of these powers on combattors\ infidelic minds

49th-the right to challenge outside the domain of soldierism and gain knowledge of this existence

50th-the right to use the vocabulary approach, when combattors sense the willingnessof successes

51st-the right to not guarantee any soldiers steadiness of learning soldierism

52nd-the right of camouflaging those fashion wears-to enlight the beauty of soldierism

53rd-the right to strike without fear

54th-if comes down to bearing a child-one must ensure the bringing up of both soldierism-the old knowledge of governance holdment of any particular knowledgerial nation

55th-by all right a soldier must not have any thought of pleasurement to no one

On this earth

56th-the right to strengthened your arms and your heart to defeat any ongoing

Atorians to any legit match arrival at any desired time

57th-if appointed or beliefs that are chosen that in the event of working for a uniform outfit, that the rule is overbombarded and casted-that the soldier must continue the life of a soldier or otherwise practice a strong withhold ever the reformation bestowed onto you

58th-it is right to act with accordance with the rule of soldierists and that minimum encouragement towards the rule—will be deemed unsettled and meaningless that the soldier would be a combattor appointment to defeatedment

59th-it is right to act both evilious and righteous in living. Know the evil desires and the good acts. A balance of both is necessary to combat the haters

60th-know that war is power and power is war. The both are equal elements when put together, can be destructive. The soldierists ways are to accomplish this goal and be triumphant over all factions before time of death

61st-the right to banish all unsuccessfulness of soldiers only to obliterate condemnation

62nd-the right to teach the elements approaching this endeavour-the consequences of enlightment and its darkness

63rd-the right to find, destroy and bring them alive. This concept comes within the societies of corrupted unsoldierist. The ones with different concepts of grasping religious fundamentals and soldierists fundamentals into a whole

64th-the ultimate challenge to command all commandments and 'all' duties opted onto a soldier. To adhere to help firmly-to keep the intelligenated mind free of all obstacles

65th-the right to show no compassion to mercy pledges and mercy acts to the human races, of the world. Merciless acts must not be prohibited in any commandments of the extension of the 1st—the MAOC.

66th-no power comes from one race and one equal strength alone. The universal world is favoured to no one equal power. Diversities would show, to lead an army, is the ultimate challenge. To win, is the ultimate force.

67th—the right to not concern with favouritisms of lusts and desires of the human races. The right to live alone and die alone, without bearance of young Blood and to see them be supreme in their ways. Unless your goals are seemingly to destroy in every generation rift

68th-the right to relieve the soldiers name and relive the soldiers life after rejuvenation of the citizens life

69th-the right to not concern with small battlery of the minded corrupters and small defensive wars

70th-the right to be closer to deaths. May it be by attempts or courageous desires

71st-the right to change all but some commandments but only to when it becomes a horror of hazard and the skills of upgrowth to the futureated. Times of radication and supremeness

72nd-the right to conformity to not consider yourself lesser value to no citizenry or higher statue in nationality

73rd-the upholdment to remember the two birth members-for bringing you onto this chaotic world, either be members of solderists or not

74th-the right of revisions-to understand that the behavours of mankind, inhibits more than one commandments

75th-interference of the commandments of the systems and the auuluumedment of living, would be catastrophic if put to the test of its behaviour

76th-the right to show courageous attitudes always when tasks are ahead

77th-remember that the ten commandments are not to governance of mans evoluted system but to that of a good living understandable by God

78th-a soldier in their performation can adhere to living towards the ten commandments-to that these commandments are rules towards living in the

[system of mans invention of governance] and which must be conquered secretly or with great power

79th-must respect the dictions of the holy scriptures to a good life-if not, well!!! a warlord you shall be?

80th-the right to distance the intelligent knacks of holy doctrines and religious factions perpetrated by 'who more righteous than who' in the system

81st-the right of knowledge to know that there is a beginning and a end and to see the beauty that [everything comes down to the beginning]

82nd-the right after a war, to be defeated to ask upon mercy and to accept loses

That the soldiers death would be painless and forgiveful

83rd-the right to let free the senses of survival and to acknowledge in any powers handed onto a soldier-we are still humans-bleed to die with vengence is not written as a commandmental rule-it is a decision of a ator alone to perform

84th-the right to not conversate to any human being other than interested persons

In the system. The order of seculsionists exists as a norm behaviour

85th-the right to be opposite than good-to show "hate" towards sectors of diversities in the world

86th-a soldier must perform the hardship of turmoil-to use the strength to bring forth your desirable needs. To any one that cheated their way to successes are abominators

87th-these rules of survival are regulation towards strong survival tactics. If any attempts are to be made to destroy a government-careful approach must be made not to inhibit these "laws of secrecy" to no citizens of any "red nations" but to be remained in its original position where it belongs. If adhering to a "dettcordian" governance a military approach would be standard at the beginning of this feat but of their own.

-88th-

The right to appointment to choose to become a leader in the world. To all

Habits to this soldierists, must endure the free power to see this power grow

And with it power and decision are made one. To history must not repeat

Itself neither must your attempts to world domination be repeated but reborn

Rejuvenated and neither it be a replica of successes. The 88th commandments

Stands separated from the 87th golden rule of the MAOC.

THE 88TH

Topic on the 88th:

All commandment do have a bearance of its true identity. It comes in one form, the form of a "flag". The power written in these flags is one to be an underminer of beliefs of unnatural forces:

The 88th is not only a formation of commandments by soldierists but a man itself trapped with a dark feeling of unwantedness of any aspect of the creation of the world and its ugliness.

The 88th strokes and the world shall fall with it alongside its nations. The beauty of unknowness is the beauty of understanding-to that, the nations formed can be destroyed by one man alone. The two hands producing the power of 88 reachment. Today, the golden 88 stands between their destruction \redemption.

Man can never destroy the 88 by a blow to the heart, his deficiency is his defiance. Deformation the true word of deficiency, the act to hardmented judgement.

Here I provide for you a belief, witness it, that all uniform warlord before me have indeed in their pocketed minds devised their own credo of commandments that supply themselves to move on with vigorousity of strength and purpose to fulfill a prophesy. Consider yourself lucky yet again.

For this is not for you to learn but observe and witness my brain at work

SCROLL{7}

Now partake to another form of commandments called the Me5, as always watch and observe

The Me5 exists from the addressing attempts of exceeding the limits to solderists activities. First the mission must be very maneuvering and quiet. Here the test of how the mind put to sketches, are thoughted out for your own survival in a specific odd nations of conflict. Hideouts are necessary so is the ability to surround any opponents journey to assassinate a soldier.

The inventions of laws made in this embodiedment system are to govern the human psyche of what are the do's and the don't. To put into a more simpler form. But the world shall not see the faith of dying in the hands of these newly formed solderists activities in the system.

Now witness the 30th commandmental rule of survival under the regime of :

METHODALICAL MESSENGERS of the MEDIATORS MANEUVORS

Of dying to contempted MISSIONS—Me5

1st-to act with accordance to the laws of civil obedience not withstanding the right of information and the right of usage of survival tactics on the civil population

2nd-to act viciously on evilous attemptors and their desires

3rd-to act bravely and calm towards acts of competition

4th-to act of camouflage to disguise appearance frequently

5th-to act silently when approach by questionable civilians

6th-to always remember the "symob"-symbol to survival and its strong motivation it brings

7th-to train always on each rising of the day to the darkened night

8th-to act of action to awareness of distortions in path of appraisals

9th-to act with accordance with the law of survival

10th-to keep judgemental acts upon soldiers who may look like downtrotten or outcasters. The world is filled with "SILENT SOLDIERS" ready till that of coming

11th-to know the paths we take to follow are not cohesive to the law of soldierisms

12th-the act to destroy attempts made by a combattor and to move ahead when tasks become too simple to bear

13th-the act to understand fully the potentiality of "life" and may obscurities coming from an individual is abnormalities and must be looked at very closely and finding means of controlment

14th-the act to support training from governmental securities, to upboost the soldierists ways of countertasking and bravery

15th-the act to guard the territories recognized as yours or for further developments or battles

16th-the act to make war against ators of different caliber-combatting for supremacy

17th-the act to lay judgement upon these sinners of the world. Crushing their every desire for power

18th-the act to speak out-to hear your voice-your anger-your hate towards mankind

19th-the act to not show compassion for no oppositions neither to make these persons feel comfortable

20th-the act to be an "inventor" "soldier" "educator". In the world, to broaden the spectrum of the mind, opening doors of horrors and disinterested paths that no mind can open

21st-the act to willingly destroy the elements on "mans interventions" and its system

22nd-the act to develop codes of languages of the soldierists ways. Ways not understandable by the citizens. To be unidentified

23rd-the act to manipulate, to cast false distributes. The art of misdirections and misplacements

24th-the act of challenge, to positions the high archy powers from soldiers of individuals not worthy of their existent positions

25th-the act to forfeit any competitors or to assigned a new combattor in place of the soldier[this act means that if the chosen "ator" is defeated a new challenge would be open to two challenges—both you and the defeated in rounds of superior skills]

26th-no combattor must take any soldier place in battle. Giving reasons are abominators to the causes. Live up to a reputation of courageousness and fearful of death

27th-the art to take forcefully as desired lust

28th-the art to be open minded and not singled minded on the aspect of the world may it be race or achievements

29th-the act to be free from any desire weakness of the system of man

30th-the act to destroy the system of governance from the beginning of time to the end of times. Dictorial and knowledgeable comes together in full force to destroy the systems of interventions

-31st-

If a cause is to be fought, it is better to annihilate billions than one. For a Cause is much greater in numbers than few and to this-no matter the Consequence of the ators desires. The quest to destroy is only and only of Mans interventions.

: The Me5 comes supremely my combator in arms: understand this

As an ideology, an ideological statement to lasting determination of survival in this rampant order in mans intervention. The disorder comes when persons of this world seems to find puzzling attributes of the history of mans evolution and comprises this knowledge with men of wisdom in the written scriptures of all holy scripts. To search for answers in these holy scripts, would lurk the seeker to nothing but more questions than answers of the troubled world. The holy scripts of "Christianity" depicts that what is seen now was predicted in the past by men of wisdom.

Nevertheless living in these troubling times can cause powerful minds to change whats been seen. Note: all uniform of war are to contribute fully in the systems of governance, finding new methods of controlment. The creation of any embodied system, to compete or multiply its power source which one eventful ear is used, to create or destroy any systems evolved. Can with take a downfall acception or deceit of the tongue to acknowledge it or not when asked.

Times of war-there's peace

Times of peace-there's hate

Times of contributions-there's battlery

Times to take action-there's rivalries

Time to make history-there's faces with no traces

For times is to make your own history, to create an honouring.

SCROLL{8}

A GOLDEN RULE: if failures persists me-are my failures and my failures Alone-to face the coincidence after tiresome taught of Analystic and treatment

This rule is a reminder that life is no joke-taking every developments seriously, introduce a survival setting in your pigmented brain of work.

On many featured notes of solderists a new at times but an old trick of desertion of elimination of any or all types of skilled military men "the art of torture". The understanding that skilled or not skilled we still bleed like the dogs we are and any surprise attack can be the end for a combattor.

To certainty, that no persons living in this world would pass away, not sharing a gift in mans domain for intelligence. The power of struggle rests on the humans occupying this earth and to this intelligence an ator looks for from all human beings, to their minds must be vast and differentiated. Long live these supremists their symbol of corruption under all intelligence.

{1}to look any other is disbeliefs

{2}to look to the future are doubts

{3}to look to master all knowledge of the human characteristics are bewilderment

{4}to look towards life of obscurities and danger are religious factions

{5}to look as life as a glory a gift to curse your own name in front of the world historic event of interest

{6}to look at your achievement is yours and no one else's own-a superior mind

A GOLDEN RULE: the gift that I am in possession of as a supremists a true Combator, is nothing short of any power but this powerful Gift will insight the ator to possibilities to endless worth's Of power at a short period of time and at a young age. The Normal beings would take in periods of ten's

This rule showcased that the power within me was meant to be there and normal beings like your self my comrade at arms, would take a lifetime to achieve, nothing short of glory ha!!!!!!!!! Ha!!!!!!!!!!.

ANOTHER GOLDEN RULE: to everytime my senses are to be tested, I see It only fit to combat any enlured treatment for ultimated destructive procurement.

HERE IS ANOTHER FOR YOU: my successes is but one alone, to when I die my successes goes with me, to not left behind to no-non creators or abominators in this world. To let my success live long and Prosper, to destroy all emotioners.

You see how greatful I am atorian: BASIC LITERACY of EGOTISM on Conquering ENEMIES DOMAINS

B.L.E.E.D

Silently the "bleed" of certainty. The knowledge of a soldier. This the soldierists knowledge will be opened to the unprescribed followers of this new periods of evolution. To bleed is knowledge of the highest. For preparation to inact for deepening solice must be ready for whats at bay. Its destructive purpose would be opened.

{1}how I an ator—picture the world in the future, is that of uncertainty

{2}how I an ator—picture the coming of the war to come to play, is that of the feelings and most important seeing all attributes to soldierists activities brings I fortune-to a limited period, so I the ator receives knowledge quickly

{3}how I an ator—picture my life in the future is that of options a-to achieve for great b-let it be given to you c-patiently wait for its showing by means of signatures

{4}how I an ator—picture my forgiveness of "hate" towards human beings-is that of only and only accomplishing depths of eliminated goals, set by the

Humans, which they have forgotten or retreated by means of their emotions

{5}how I an ator—picture my gifts of successes, if ever it reaches the point of not returning it to its source, for its own destruction, to it carries the "host" to un bodily challenges which the body can no longer but not to die, is that of and only of.

{6}how I an ator—picture my success being tested and my defeated by a less compatible opponent-is that of unapproachable and remember that there are "many battles but there's only one war"

{7}how I an ator—picture myself turning my success to powers of controlment of all behaviours of the world inventions ever thoughted from the evolution of the equilibrium time. Feelings of unhuman characteristics and knowledge of attempts that no other ever achieved would perish in silence.

A GOLDEN STATEMENT: it is not a war-till there is a persistent approach, then realization are shown of the combattors mind towards power of soldiers and towards a living Soldier.

ANOTHER GOLDEN RULE: singular positions of agendas of my power of success shall be a curse to you and your generations. To not let your powerful gift stand at one positions. To destroy all humans at positional ranks and to own it.

HERE IS ANOTHER FOR YOU: as an individual ator, it counts a lot when success comes from an individual, rather than a grouping, supporting your success. When in turn ever learning your techniques of skills goes with you, so does your spark of entertainment.

These rules are to give guidance to visionaries of any ator who wishes to observe and learn.

ANOTHER GOLDEN RULE: failures are not the ators way of option-for failures are considered a "curse" for us-the atorian are triumphantly supreme over "mind power". The power of concentration, that comes with mind power and for we fall numerously without a "feat of glory". Then we shall depart from this gift and return to the human spectrum of life, the condemnation for the truth.

This book was written to remind us-nothing is impossible, the mind can perceive whatever it wishes and to this warlord, well? He would destroy every confidence made my men-hidden by men-guarded at their brain. For the system we live today are failures made by history, made by man. Understand this philosophies my comrade and witness the prophesy.

SCROLL{9}

OBSERVE THIS: The ator carries the wickedness, death, annihilations and peaceful emotions, displayed upon the beings of this world. To what is let out is whats inside of an ator. But there can only be "one" uniform warlord of this generation. The generation where both strengths and intelligence goes hand in hand in the destruction of this force circling this world. For this force is a sign of lowerbility of self. The underachieving of life's meaning, displayed by heavy emotions non of this world.

For this force must be captured and put to the test of difficulty and maneuvering. The system challenges us yet again. "what do we do?"

We—the atorian

Destroying—capturing

Entertaining—toiling

Escaping—planning

Fearlessness—competitions

Power—war and the desire to hold the sources of the two together. The source of two singular strength. That can never be put together and its trouble capturing it and securing it—singular strength—singular strength

{power}—{war}

To these two strength one can deceit the other when the human mind captures its strength. For the human CIB-is still fuctioning with the attributes of products to feed the brain.

FOR WHAT ONE LACK-ONE MUST FIND AND INHERIT

UNPORPORTIONAL TALENTS-THAT ARE NON BEFORE SEEN.

For that is a golden rule of an ator. To not all ators are born with extravagant gifts, to there are many similarities of the world. To see and make observations to defeat and move on. Ators objective are to be singular to gifts and achievements, to be solely viscous when non-combattors tries of copymasterfully.

Let me show you here how I think and what motivates me daily and in you mind ask yourself, is this the kind of thinking I adopt

What is done is done, what was yesterday, which was told today, which affects tomorrow, which inhibits stimuli of either courage or fear. To this I say what was done was done, who hears my name shall fear my name, hear me now!!! Those who see my name shall scream at my name, let it be known. I shall make a soldiers "pledge of allegiance" that I, the true and only warlord in this 21st century shall make the beliefs of man and men, to hear my name and fear my name. To I am no longer in apprenticeship with any other human, for their stupidity is noted. To who can fool me, I have written, I have understand every form of intelligent ideas man can make unto this world.

You think you can perform any of "work of trickery" without me knowing. To this I say, to I shall go into the deep escapes of the human mind where I can be better feared by man and their trickery—it has begun.

SCROLL{10}

My colleague at arms, remember that what you witness here today, is a unique time for you. Remember this and rekindle it well: have you ever heard about :

PROPHESY THEORIES: this is where a mind of a being knowingly knowing that such being has a purpose in life, an extraordinary one in fact and in case of ensuring it, does such being then decide to find out what is their strongest feats. Working tirelessly on such gifted feats allow the mind to then create conjectures and wild theories. Here is one for you.

REGEMIC ATTITUDES

1ST ORDER TO ATTENTION

Vengeance is yet again upon me this ator. One chosen combattor trying to dictate another, unnoticeably a "resilient" testimonials.

1st presiding order-I am who I am, don't question my intelligence

1st commanding order-I am who I am a soldier, no doubt, of the 88th commanding allegiance to be created into the real of the world

1st allegiance order-be all I can be, no more no less, to survive amongst the greatest—amongst the cowards

1st attacking order-I must show my strength and create a system unlike any of this world and still possess the capability to destroy it.

-Creation of the 1st order-the order recognizes that I a uniform warlord is a

Representation of my own uniformed organization must not nor never believe in

Such arm to save my life when in harms way. To this is a order of declaration

That this book written by the ator himself must be used when in frontal attacks by

Any{1} uniformed officers of a government {2}civilians of a system who are

Volunteers to a uniform {3} combattors of a true cause {4} foreign Interventionists. I must be brave and must be able to destroy.

Oh!!!!!!!! Yes my comrade, now you know, little by little you read, you will find out more about me. Oh!!!!!!! Yes I am a member of my own uniform organization arm that is not in existent entirely but it is in the making in the works of the world.

Now, I represent a new order and the new order is a upgrade to the new combattors at large and disguise: survility—survility—survility.

1st order to survility: recognizable by me the "ator a true combator"—To this the human emotional behaviours conquers all logic of human controlment which of course undoubtedly, is made up of human emotions. Nonetheless when the emotions known as men of hate, which is recognizable to the human eye, which is then an action, can be overwhelming to the point. Where such emotions can become a powerful ally to a human just cause, to survive and to maintain "survility".

Note that when a man's hate is so powerful due to ones dislikes of another or others, it builds a confidence to remain in that position. To defeat hate itself or the ones who are in possession of certain actions, that none the less are portrayed as actions, is a trait one shall not ask for if you're not ready for the tasks ahead.

2nd order to survility: the true solderism and its attributes states this the 21st century, every individual tries or is trying to be that perfect "soldier". Want to survive and for this the true combattor must apply the era for a:

8 guerilla warfare: the 8 guerilla warfare is simply a system one must adopt to achieve maximum fellowship from untrained marksmanship to solderism. Firstly the commandments that goes with such warfare and it states:

1st—for the soldier to want this, such soldier must understand all limits and unlimitation to his strengths both physical and idealists wise.

2nd-such soldiers must remained disciplined even if such soldier uncovers his face and appears gullible around factions.

3rd-such soldiers must copy notes at least full coverages of the world effects and its non existence. Praises are that of latter to come however such notes must be of your own thoughts and not of others.

4th-such soldiers if pleases, represent any factions of system but should not forget the meaning to such life.

5th-such soldier must believe in himself from such notes such shall write. No soldier must not betray or burn such written notes, for this shall be an abomination to this highest degree. Such degree shall be meant with annihilation of self.

6th-such soldier must remained fully aware and fully trained for any battle to come.

7th-such soldier must never reveal such motives or either such purpose of definition, that may sound a blur to the human ears. Until such one shall meet a gifted spirit within such being, such shall be related to and be meant on guard.

8th-such soldiers must not be blunt, knowledge about everything, something, all things are imperative to further survival unto the futureated.

9th-such soldiers must become more than human in thought and in ways. become a nonexistent being, living amongst existence people. Meaning that, such persons shall move like "spirits" living amongst the living.

10th-such soldiers must always remember {survival comes first, anything other Than that comes after}.

11th-such soldiers must remain vigilant on the emotional behaviour. For emotions cannot be taught it can only be learnt. After such learning one control its behaviour that triggers off impulses from the brain unto the synapses of the muscles attached unto the bones for movement. Non the less it can be controlled by manipulative decision making.

Oh!!!!!!!! What a beautiful command, read this now you insignificant human being and admire and learn.

2 ONE SOME AND THEN MORE SOME

The 88th beliefs: Welcome to the traits that one can develop due to its creative emotional inhibitions. When amongst those that your creative mind puzzles, then such a mind shall be brought to a test to masterfully. When the mind feels insecure about future movements then such mind becomes the "enemy". The one you then become up against.

Knowledge is important but to this warlord, it must present itself.

A SCREAMING MOMENT: Sometimes feel hurtful due to who I am, what I do And to whom. I love battles,

I love war but those That seek help
and those who knows nothing about
War, prophesying warlike behaviour,
interrupts it Like, figuring the mind of
a "warlord"—you can Never know
the next move.

END NOTES: to this chapter represents my pledges, unknown to man for a Period. Let it be now known, that I have many battles with soldiers, with or Without my caliber, that for them to spread around to hit me at every Direction, to distant myself from who I am, what I do and to whom I Represent. My atorians, shall be the first amongst men to understand how men Are and how all of them deceitfully conceive, their plans to achieve, the Unbelieve. But soon gets grubble with a sought of fought, never thought, ever Existed from a single "nought". What is a nought?. A nought is an action, that must never be seen by a rival combattor until the Final match is approachable. This action must not even be seen leaving the Creator to reach the combattors side of power. And for this action to exist, it must Not ever be existed for some poachers to inhibit its strength, It must be left Within the spokes of the mind and must be seen amongst other ators worthy to See such magnificence. A nought consists of one of many plans to be created to destroy the words ofMans intelligence. Their intelligence, that is stored. For this nought would Become a new way of life similar to military lifestyle and isolation of these Uniformed premises.

Chorus: when soldier comes and he comes alone, you do no more but show up with more, am I seeing thick straight there's more to seek faith, loose and undone your going to walk out here a right hand God saint, best of you think death going to be a sweet licker—licker—licker!!!!.

You should sing this my learned friend, as we end this courageous, spit swallowing, nail biting, cold sweating—ART OF CONQUERINGMENT.

TO CONQUER TO RULE—TO CONQUER TO RULE—TO DESTROY!!!!

CHAPTER X

The art to intellect

SCROLL{1}

Oh!!!!!!!!!! How I would put your brains on a platter and experiment on your deficiency of the use of your intelligence to that of mines.

Now you ator are about to learn about my intellectuality and witness how powerful such is and learn how, one with such power, needs to portray a figure like this, to whenever those who believe they posses similar traits-must crush them, must pulverize them.

Your signature is needed for this testimony art to begin_______________________________.

Welcome yet again, my combator who is willing to witness the prophesy days of the ART TO INTELLECT.

Let us distinguish here, a great difference between an elder and a junior in relation to intelligence proportionalities: let us begin.

It is noticeable, that there can be a "father" and a "son" and a "elder" and a "junior". The positions we believe, we hold over others of less superiority, due to little reignment over the earth, or incompetence to solve its treasures. A father is just a man, as everyone else and no more. Regardless, of the fear or joy instilled within a son. As a son is a human with little reign on his shoulders of feats, with little knowledge of the world-regardless of a father, can never indulged in meetings of confrontations and admit that "fathers" are more intelligent in wisdom than a "son". To this, it can never be a "son" which may posses a unique gift, untouchable by any man in this world. Even the father's faith that it is not true. The world is different, when the man of yesterdays, lives his lives without little reign of accomplishment, the man of tomorrow has to double his feats of knowledge to better the man of the futureated or "tomorrow till". This means that when the son becomes more wisdomic, than the father and this it shall be. For man has finally admit that "intelligence" is more powerful than their respect of their elders. No matter the careful choice of a man's mate to create a perfect child, this child becomes a successor over his elders and competitions among his peers. The impossible are no longer there, when a soldier produces a thought and powerful and impregnable to the societal system. It is said that "elders" needs to be respected, due to their longevity and their period of understanding life before you. Not so—the young ones are being left to think for themselves, some may posses a greater skill to learn faster than others, to this help, is needed for the less adaptable but none is given to the continuous forceful impact of information with less rest of body.

An imbalance can be shown and cannot be control but must be continued until a powerful force can be required to emit a lesser type of information unto them. When this is created, human beings introduce "laws" of governing themselves, to different limits. Their different values and then their different work positions are introduce as we have spoken of its existence before. This is the creation of different ideology of man and what makes them different within the societal system-so it is written-. What makes this child to adopt more efficiencies than others; during these "educational intellects", is it their biological structures or their own efficiency? Then, only their efforts can bring about a change within the structures of the world and its feats to be conquered and "tamed". To these thinking only evolves their strengths of conquerisms. It is noticeable that leaders today are deciding their bases of rivalries on anger than on intelligent decision. The leaders of tomorrow, has to clean up their mess and move, making decisions on problems affecting their governing over the subjects, on what are problems facing tomorrow. Was not seen yesterday, which was today and tomorrow was never seen and not created by mans decision made yesterday. But the inhabitants, inability, to survive the fierceness of the worlds energies and its age.

Yes my friend it came a time where my intellect amongst the masses of the elders was under scrutiny, at a young braveheart I show signs of combatness and courage to explain my ideology but I never waiver to their dislikes instead I consume every loathsome words and build me a confidence that now they run and hide when my name is called: ha!!!!!!!!!!!!! ha!!!!!!!!!!!!!!!! ha!!!!!!!!!!!

SCROLL{2}

Here is another for you: man has become a symbol of weakness, men do all works for a man of high statue, look and speak degrading to represent true companionship but men has become a symbol of themselves ready to be destroyed, by the elements of the world's demeanor.

If I the true warlord, knows within myself that I the true ator has in my possession a truly unique wisdomic source of power, then I must know it's for a purpose of truth, then I must find it and its challenges and its limits of strengths to if I don't, then my combattors will grow and produce multifolds of chaos amongsts man and their limited knowledge. Until carnage is created which I am called upon to destroy and if I may utter "for its strength has grown due to my ignorant behaviour of not creating a "combattor" towards its strength and its beginning period."

If I may utter a similarity "I must discover and produce this form of information on true soldierisms, together with my own knowledge and this shall produce a

"combine strength" to challenge this "new reborn system" which has lived through "my era" and are willing to survive another". Due to this new reborn system, many ideas of man must be combined together on "one entity". To create this reborn system due to its growing knack of intelligence to survive. Which gives man of today a figure of disdain power that is unstoppable and courageous like no other. due to this system, it can prove useful to our cause, so as when the "newly revoluted warlord" challenges this reborn system, all the ideas of man are challenged as well. When defeated they shall give me additional strength over the minds of man, for a long period of time until new developments are reinvented. But to this, it may not occur for a long time, giving me time to create a new system to whenever and whoever it shall return. To this waiting of a new era is upon us, to then we defeat the chaotic system, is very risky and dangerous and more beings would be devoured.

When there is a destiny to be done, then let it be so, let it be done.

So as to give the atorians of tomorrow an ease of waiting and challenging his own being of doubling his efforts and strength and by doing the unthinkable. asking for help by the normal man that only dictates and contribute all their efforts by being "critics" to all common cause. Benefital to their own well being as well as their offsprings. And for the human dominance, a chance to greater their intelligence and support all forms of movement to create or recreate inventions for the futureated.

We must all perform all duties, either it be dangerous in the future "we must", to this is the only way of knowing the mind, which must be used to its fullest potential and ideal, to be putted forth to its extent.

This my expedient ator is as deep you can really get, remind me that a reward shall be given unto me for this deepening words of closeness, we are not close till you become hypnotized and bow down to this intelligence.

I present to you a little subject to wonder the mind about in this scroll, sometimes its good to explore the depths of information, this scroll will allow you to accept no other:

What happens when those without power, then decide to search for some, only for means of protection, this creates a "war on a battlefield". It may be on political grounds, or on governance or on rulement over people of local statues or foreign. Thus entering the creation of two words "conquerable and defeater". Thus creating a new empire that, every things always comes down to the beginning, the beginning of mans system that there shall be kings amongst men, rulers over men, one always hold all power. Power of politics, power of governance, power of law & rulement, power of competitions.

Here you see that all powers man holds today were all discovered and invented by one power of entity. To this being, their only intentions, was to discover the depths within the mind and after discovering such depths, would use it to explore the wonders of the world and all the effects onto mankind. To this the man of the 21st century are the most powerful man of history, due to a lot of information that were passed on by the intelligenated mind of those before, whose intentions were to better mankind in the future and of cost themselves.

What is greatly understandable, is when an intelligent mind creates an existent that are so powerful than the existent system which then becomes a main attraction and attracts a lot of attention by means of a great invention called "satellite". Let me broader the mind here my ator on this device:

A transport medium used on all devices to transport wavelengths on inventions that then after captured, transmit messages from any point necessary, to any point at its necessary "needs". These needs may include "information" on developments surrounding any cabinet meetings involving government representatives around their private capacity, knowledgeable it can become. Needs may include the use of advanced technologies and devices transportable or stationary, that uses the invention of the satellite medium to source or generate such power to inventions, that are slaves to its already functional existence. Such inventions are already existent or created wholly. The satellite then on reaching to its capabilities adds additional power to the already existent inventions.

These inventions uses the power of the satellite to function, to many inventions are indeed "slaves" to the existence of the satellite which may become a deterrent if ever destroyed. The most powerful buildings in the world are those that functions and maintains the order of the satellite by means of a control system, surrounded by a brain base. This system must be powerful due to the ingenious minds that created such inventions and the minds that control its power now.

Here is another mind searching mind boggling attempt to enter the mind of no elimination:

During the generation of man, man has captivated all ideas which have been brought to one conclusion, that there shall be one type of high expressionated thinking and personalizing degree of living. To such living has come from the European way, where other individuals have continued the way of their old living, therefore creating a havocking understanding between a "new & old system of living, thus creating hidden agendas whilst working alongst the existing system but obtains a different view that are told about until a creation has been created and a creator shows an appearance.

To I, this warlord writes, the uniform never begets me, for I have written this with much favour and honour, live my life with honour and to die honourably and nobly.

There can be no room for trickery or deceit, not when knowledge is involved. When knowledge lacks communications between such powers as the people chosen for government and the people chosen to live under such power. To this no matter what type of government are portrayed by such nations, by means of coup-e-tat or by power of their constitutional rights to vote, they are always chosen. Chosen to be appointed, choose themselves to be appointed and as such "citizens" can either

-choose the ones to be appointed legally or illegally by interfering or non interference—or-

Consider choosing themselves to be under such "governance", either way, the potentially innocent "citizens" cannot be trusted due to:

{1}ideals are personally recognized as that of your own, on the contrary, under a government ideals, can become one whereas

the regular citizens, all feels the burden either if high positionary or of low status. Their voice always becomes one and due to this, the ultimatum can be heard that citizens do not need to be in a position where a entity can rule over them and due to this, the realization are shown, a new entity becomes created thus bringing forth words like "terrorists, militias, left wing radicalists to support such entity.

{2}humans beings, when a system choose to rule, may not go in occurrences with such rule, thus adding to additional woes to such system which are controlled by human beings themselves, from the same nation as those who approve ruleship from such a system. And to those who disapprove—well!!!!!!—a combattor is very well created. Thus adding to more woes, thus adding to a system outside of an existing system to gain income from such system and not of their own. This produces more woes and more conflict between the "disapprove citizens" and the existing system which survive only by the "approve citizens" collectively on the account of both parties of such a government system, thus creating deaths.

Occasionally, the disapprove citizens becomes part of the approve citizens only by means of trickery, on behalf of competing against the existing system which still institute laws of governance on the land.

Competition would only be possible, when the disapprove citizens holds enough powers over the approve citizens who resides in such positions, around such citizens, who engage in "free expressions" and to enough resources, to create a system of themselves to safe guard their free expressions, against all forces that such a government has in their possession.

To such disapprove citizens, who lurk outside of an existing system for income or for other means personally and diversely, may not have the possible ideas that these citizens do still reside amongst, an existing system, thus creating more chaos. It can be noted that their systems, non can create no matter what format they may be in, can have the power to "interlude" amongst the mind of the people who resides amongst a "weak governance" of a system, which can hold limited amount of strength over such a nation. Thus, resulting to new creation of systems by the common man in the pinnacle workforce of a governing nation, which resembles the system which it came from. Which then become a new existing force within an existing system which idealists may be different and unique.

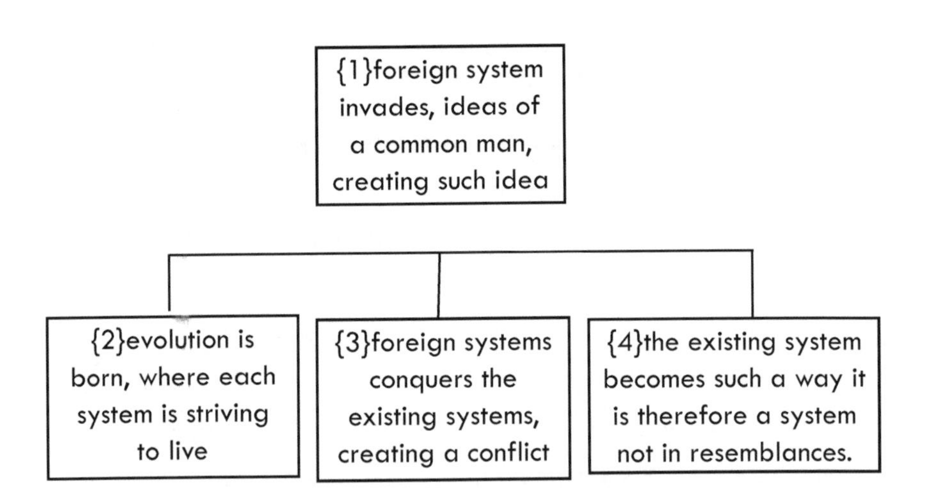

The only possible way each of the two systems can survive is by:

Human intervention: strength and forces, counts only, when the amount of figures of each individuals are represented and mutated ideas, becomes a reality and brought forth to the real of the nation.

Unwise to keep two systems in existence, when this occurs, citizens becomes more powerful than even their works, even the laws they have created becomes mindless.

Wow!!! what a rendition my atorian friend but understand this:

Here you have witness that foreign intervention never took part in their own destruction but of the willingness of the citizens, to search for other sources of power outside their already chosen system, lurks for serious downfall.

Citizens must never dishonour your works in creation of good governance, no matter the few disapproval citizens who searches to disrupt such a system, by means only of themselves and of their personal vendettas. Is it to be told, that a man must suffer the burden due to ones man diligence not to perform his works of rational analogy. Or to capture a mans happiness and cast it out to the winds, like if it's the broken old leaves that looses their grip from the branches and ceases to exist no more.

Can this remind the man, that power can only so much exist within the grasp of a mortals hand until that day, the hand is fragile enough to not hold its sources, which has solely contribute to that individuals wealth for that profound periods. To this power, may be in a different form, once seen before by the use of a pertinent source before it was finally free, due to another's intelligent brain to adapt to its cause, to enslave once caught, to this we can acknowledge the importance of :

{1}obtaining power, {2}searching for falling power, {3}creating a new power,

{4}seizing and capturing its power. These human flesh you call them seem to be of greater importance than we may think.

SCROLL{3}

-A prophesy of one:

A dream which becomes an idea, then becomes an ideal thought, which then is created to the world which is then created into a system, which is then used to obtain finance or to employ the destitute knowledge that are not profitable. But to the extent without it, ever leaving the brain which it means, it is not created as yet but it lurks entirely around the hemisphere of the brain. To this, can all dreams reach their final destination, which means finally completed, to which can be ready to explore into the world of man or better yet show the real persons who beholds such a dream or ideas.

-A prophesy of two:

That I this uniform lover of a warlord, promises to create an entity and make such existence present unto the real of the world, no matter how chaotic it may be. It should be a reckoning, aptitudal force in history.

How to create a wrath?—a wrath known to such solderists livers are as it is seen to achieve the impossible even desiring all measures to achieve such. To destroy what is built and create, what its, in on one minds agenda.

-A prophesy of three:

We have spoken many on the beliefs to create a military state of anthems, most disciplined "disciples" to its cause.

The tricks of traits: discipline is discipline for I the atorian, cannot and will not bestow emotions unto the regular infidels of man, for why should I fight for you as well as, for me. When such as you would not take time to accomplish feats on your own. For the world, my people, is one that this conqueror cannot trust or either trust to fight my fight, for my open agenda shall be:

WHATS INSIDE OF ME SHALL NOT BE BESTOW OUT OF ME, AND WHATS OUT OF ME SHALL NOT BE PUT INTO ME.

For my blood must never be spilled over my opponents, neither shall their force of actions be printed to my body to destroy what' s in me. Due to this I shall make and create a fitting machine for the world, my body in perspective. To this i say, for the night as well, I cannot trust, for more fierce concentrative action of defense must be inhibited for further survival. For my sight is being lessened in the night than my full oversight during the day. Due to this disadvantage my "survival skills" shall be my weapon against it—so it is said, so shall it read.

-A prophesy of four:

I the "atorian d combatorian"-which I have announced you and the rest of the populists who seeks a dominance in their intelligence to which they think they might have as a "atorian" also. Acknowledge this:

And only this, I am not angry at the world, for what it is but angry at myself for being so self absorbed, with all the attributes that are available to offer. And to this, my conscious mind has strayed away from all discipline elements of controlment of self first, and then other continuous action will offer. For what it is, it is, what was meant to be. To if my mind is not control, certain elements are battlering, then so shall I listen, even many countless defeat has followed. To one day such mind will become useful to other forces, within their blockade of Kabul systems or either unfamiliarity would and cause damage, to any selected created system one may execute.

It is noted; that there can be two equal powers of beings within one system, so advanced is this system that such two powers cannot destroy itself or each others being to survive. To such powers remains equals but such powers welcome the challenge of having subjects below them, in control of other subjectments. Then, there are those that certain beings are meant to have knowledge, to control certain person's ability to use such powers over combatants. To this is notably known throughout the history of men. Factor known as "human error". It sounds tricky but note that what is mentioned above are equal, most known knowledge are. And because of this, certain persons become repellant towards eachother, having a dislike of eachother due to similarities in such contained powers.

Prophesy, prophesying, prophetic—I seem to be in an art towards this. Give me an input, how do you think about my intellectuality now. Its but just a few, more to come. Place your idea about what you understand so far:

____

____

____

____

____

____

____

We are about to enter the lifestyle of these populists and my views it shall be witnessed. Here is another for you ator:

To no longer do combatants of both side fight like the years of the past where all settlements are fought on a normal battlefield. For now the 21st century the ideas of such combatants crosses with the "unarmed" civilians thus creating these uncertain lifestyle all over the world. The world has become a scene of mayhem, where even if knowledge, is apprehensive about innocent minds being caught by such combatants, must die like "soldiers", like they have so highly expressed themselves "for cowards they are". To what is now the will of civil man to make bones within this world by such as their ideas. The unintelligent minds of the rebellious civilians, destabilize the stable system, then and only then such rulement by the rebellious will become short and sudden, due to other enemies or combattors, who prefers their role over such landmass or nation.

Such as wars, will be considered and planned, where knowledge is applied, when such successor is seen. Wouldn't such soldiers have to bestow a rulement likewise as the destroyed existing system before? "To why does man follow their intentional emotional unstableness and not of prophetic individuals?" The way of how and why man shall behave, just to prevent what may occur. Man!!!!! Leave the prophesy for me, humans beings in charge of systems portray a weakened dislikes.

SCROLL{4}

A THEROLOGICAL WONDERMENT THAT GATHERS INTELLECTUALITY
:

Understand this: that there is a warzone that is functioning outhere {the real of the world works or works of the world}. It survives on our own uncontrolled emotional behaviour, which can only be displayed unto another human being who has to face confrontations of such behaviours. And to this, the continuous flow of action between the two comes from the other being who has no choice to defend his life and because of this, each individuals thrives in its existence, for the world would never see peaceful days. For man ideas has achieve the inevitable, dreaming of this day the 21st century, when individuals themselves would hold more power than king, queens, appointed leaders. The will is very much alive.

For war began between:
Leaders—combats—leaders
Nations—combats—nations
The combined of nations—combats—nations aligned
Individuals—combat—individuals

For man thinks alike for such feats to change. One must have a unique power to change the minds of the combattor himself called man.

Witness now two theories in display analyze it and ask yourself the profound meaning to such:

Man destroys all works of men where no signs of God is near. To this their minds has become to think for this one shall not intimidate the civilians for this gun don't sleep well with us, for it is government own-part time own-job preference own—for government guns don't sleep well with us-bewarned- civilians sleeps with theirs for fun, for joy to become annoy to become astounded. A system must always be astound when it comes with "security" one must remember uniformed officers are always regarded as combatant towards the civilians. The civilians that solely want no affiliations with any dominant system regardless if its democracy or otherwise-be real it is real therefore think effective, they must for if they do not this atorian would. the battle continues with:

Civilians—can create their own system by approval of a appointed leader, be it may be existed within the existing system or otherwise non-existence or null within the eyes of the system.

Uniformed officers—do represent an existing system towards the people and their representative bodies.

You can witness how deceitful civilians are to the regimic uniform. Where pride follows entirely but this shall change when I prophesy a coming of a powerful uniform.

The theory of an idealist on all government organizations {1}:

Many first world nations has all but "humanitarian" output on their mind but one aspect in all of this corrupted regimic systems is the amount of "immigraters" that sign on the dotted line. The function that this created system works is third world citizens visits or either migrate from these systems, to the very best on, first world lavishly luxuries, before them but to admire the created ideas of adventurous creations such man can make and display among themselves and think of them as God amongst men, beasts among the untamed.

If one shall go a certain way, all that is seen before them is not what is displayed on their own people who toil to be best but fall short along the way. All men can be great creators of the many but who shall these men wait on, redeemers, philosophers. Why live amongst the creators, when such person themselves have not or can never contribute a continual of creation or discovered one on their own terms.

The wars today in this 21st century, are due to more a political regime than to their own philosophy. The world is blind, for they do not see what befalls on them, beside them. May it be in front, just to pitch a glance to utter a word of concern. Flattery shall never get the better of me.

To survival tactics, gets all head going over any movements by enemy combatants or friendly at heart. The days will see that the second in command shall conquer and rule powerfully but what is noticeable in many domains, the system of the law namely "police seeks power of their own over the "military as well the fictional creative ideas of these film makers, shall destroy all demise of over thinking on your own account.

The reality is this, power struggling and mistakes to create all three {3} powers and place them among, to know each other, to help each other, to keep each other, while in war but such persons when left to discover, left to grow amongst the many hands that touches it. Soon will "sour" its taste, because the three then becomes power stricken hungry: the military, the politicians, the judiciary. No longer can they feel patriotisms. The mind takes control over their intelligence, their duty, their responsibility is left behind or either destroyed with all their ways of even getting caught. A creative system is introduce within an existing system which already exists and serve its people, for this is its true responsibility. These representation of these prestigious system, then become a representation of what befall us.

For what if a government collapses or is destroyed, will civilians who create these systems to survive be breaking the law of the land. For there is no existing systems but a system that had existed. But to create a new one not withstanding that one has failed, would these civilians who would be living comfortably allow such a creation. And by this time such sectorialization, separatisms of the country by groups, religious background or either full fledge patriot groups.

You will love this: theory of an idealists {2}:

Power can exists in "one" but undecided whether "good" or "bad" they make of it.

To this the true ator says: Words and conversations that are brought to my pigmented mind must be written down to bring some truth to what I may think of it. I am neither good or bad but in between the greater forces, ha!!!!!!! ha!!!!!!! I must add.

I was born to hold power, the "immaculate" divine, that changes the "will" of me and the some of men, that have tried to overcome its power "but what is this power?" this divine power to {rule over men and not rule for man} the many of men and misery they carry as men.

To this I say: one day it would be acclaimed from the west a man of boyish figure would take the mantle with his ideas and forge on alliance with the many of men for some reason, will heed new accomplishments due to the depleted, diminishing look and lack of respect namely "the uniform" and such man shall therefore hear such cry and on its presence and instead build a "system" out of an "existent one" but more powerful, forceful, it shall be and man as we know it would feel a presence of power unnotably.

That is why my soldiers, one shall always keep his ideas till that day shall arise where the mantle shall rest on you and you shall already know what must be done. So dream your dream, live your dreams and devour it like its inferior appetizers for such courage and valor goes a long way. To this I say.

Theory of an idealist {3}

Can I ever serve a country of degenerates, those that knows nothing as they parade themselves loathfully and guards such emotions willfully and the people are barbarians to their very cause. None the less, the people love to make money at any cost. But knowledge of the battlery and wars yet to come, they must know if not, they need not seek, then "doom" it shall look upon them. One must know and understand the power of the "mind" which is more powerful than anything. Put the ideas of man with the emotions of man, the two combinations can be lethal. One can make the idea of the mind and recreate an existent system to a more powerful one by just duplicating its strength to unporportional measures.

Understand theories are theories, however if the mind wants to go so far as entering the depths of elimination and introducing a prophesy to it due to your belief that you an "atorian" has a purpose in life—well by all means "ANNIHILATE" but leave some for me—I love to "PULVERIZE". HA!!!!!!!! HA!!!!!!!!!HA!!!!!!!!!!

SCROLL{5}

We are about to enter a very indepth intellect period here. Be all eyes and witness it yet again: my topic is simply this:

Where is the position of the military, the use of it and where it hopes to be:

Were all are lost, were new recruits are needed in honour to protect their beloved nations and to always keep in mind that their nation is the greatest. The most powerful, to all counts down to "honour" "respect". What has our lives came down to; it shall remain a fortune where nations have no conflict to that of the "Europeans"-the major conquerors of this world. The effects of wars especially world wars are that systems are mutated, the usage of weapons by citizens for wrong doings or greedy purposes. The terrorists are all examples of "walls of terror wars". For men who create them "die with their success" not ever knowing how to defeat or challenge their success until their success reaps out good fortunes for nations at interested heart. For that was the history during wars but the effect is catastrophic.

For no leaders today knows how to control these soldiers with rage and hate. For they are too much with enormous strength and intelligence of battlery, to which is now known as the

AGES OF MUTATED EVOLUTIONS: The 21st century where strength and intelligence goes hand in hand as the beginning where battlery was found, which has been mutated centuries and centuries over and over, whom "life" is regarded is nothing. To much of battles produce mentality of beliefs to their prays. Which is about to get worse in the future. Many soldiers believe in murdering millions\billions of masses and for their own belief they should be let alone till they see their old age.

For this shall never be the way of "soldierism". You die and die in battle and no where else but the "battlefield" now called {territorial battlery} which would be written in historical writings. For the preservations of the past and knowledge to the future. To these history gives man another way of expanding their intelligence to limits. Where dying is more expensive than before, where wealth and money determines a nations plan of action. Where powerful nations with enormous wealth perceives their eyes, what they see is what you see—manipulation and the third world nations fight for little that they do have, not wanting help from the "powerhouses"

For not all powerhouses has all the resources, some may be disperse off or not in huge amounts. A similarity is shown with an army, for not all armies has the same resources for this is the true meaning of battlery. The anticipation for the results, the meaning of rivalries the happiness to "die" with honour.

To where does military stand with government. To the laws are written that government are the creators of the military. To the military are put are slaves to their masters. Note there atorian: The military is a system of it own with no creation but the man who decides upon survival over "rulement". For the world would look upon military way of life, when the war is upon and its effect it would have of leaders.

For even if there is a balance of both leadership of the highest rank to the highest person of government. How long does it last? "Why do nations use military to overthrow a government and their leader governing a nation?" Why can politicians get rid of politicians in the use of government policy whether different in ruleship. To they are all forms of government.

{1} there are many forms of government, to know one thinks that democracy is the best forum of ruleship.

{2} despite using a form of government whether different, one does not trust the interest of diplomacy to any types of government.

{3} a government needs the military and the citizens who can volunteer to become a soldier, parliamentarian, voter.

To this is the weakest link to a nation, the trio of dominance; for unlike man, man can achieve the goal of any three but books is what separates the three and the knowledge that comes with it. To this is a remembrance why there are sepratists in powerhouses. The vigilantes, these militias, for these movements has one rule, the usage of what was thought unto them by their own governments and the neglects that comes with it

Serving a government is always betrayal to any battlery men at arms

And protecting "voters" not civilians.

Voters: are the most manipulative citizens in any government ruled nation. They decide who their chosen one is. For this is only considered in a democratic system. The government changes, constitution changes but the military is upgraded by rules and condition under the most prestigious outfit security in the world. The uniform whose jobs are to protect the citizens\voters.

For I the uniform warlord, support any outrageous group fighting for their place in history. The men at arms under battlery law. So is it with religion and solderism, for no soldier must never condone to scriptures portraying their beliefs onto solderism acts in the world. Said it many times "soldierism" has no place in the kingdom of Gods. To solderism are a product of mans invention of rulement or system. It is the use of us on earth to make decisions on such rulement.

Oh!!! What knowledge that has been bestowed unto you about the military wanton wastage of its true power—the introduction of good governance has silenced this dormant sleeping beast from ever awaking. Witness that some individuals showing characteristics of a leader has broken the shackles of this beast we called "the uniform" and has used it to their demeanor. Ask yourself why did they not use the ambience of "politics" to achieve their goals fully. Oh yes!!!!!! They did use such an entity but behind the mask wore another face. And the political arenas, was shock because such an individual had the power of: intellect of rulement, intellect of knowing how to follow first, intellect of the uniform and a vision that surpass any individuals. Always remember whenever you may be in possession of a gift of intellectuality, use such a gift to enter the demise of the system work force plenty.

I will bestow unto you a pledge an atorian pledge: read it out loud:

Our atorians aim are to be more than just human. For this is what keeps us going, keep us alive, give us strength. Us atorians duties are to recognized that human error is part of us, for we are still human but our living is different for we depend on the usage of the c.i.b. and solderists activities, dominating all factorial bodies. For our aim are to win all battleries, to lead us to the inevitable "war" but to accomplish that, we must use our bodies to produce friction against all rivalries.

For failures are never our options—it's a curse—it's the down ness of self, historically.

For never trust an "Ator"—uniform warlord, we can be both good and evil minded. For the holy doctrines rest in the middle {we choose, we believe would better our cause to successes}. For our goals are to succeed.

SCROLL{6}

A SOLDIERS AFFIRMATION ON GATHERED INFORMATION:

{1} Soldiers who you know, you know nothing of them, soldiers who you now discovered their existence you learn from them but do not share secrets with them. Soldiers who you do not know but see them in the existence of the world and share moments of you, may be age similarities or just in existence together, you watch them shadowy, and learn from their triumphants and their defeated moments. For every information that is being brought to the intelligenated mind, posses such information and examine its contents then introduce a new system to the real of the world to harness, the processed information whilst your new ideals, is also surviving to stay functionable in the world.

So the only way your new ideas came in existence of man are due to the information you as an intelligent being posses. And because of such relations, one can survive within the spectrum of the combative minds of man, while others uses their "critic" lines to condemn others beliefs in knowledge during conversational moments and prefers their knowledgeable ideals.

But in this 21st century, one can only win combative conversations only when such being possesses more knowledge on the topic than the combattor themselves. If then, two combattors possesses the same amount of knowledge, then the introductions of a different knowledge, are harnessed and introduced. The knowledge of survival tactical skills of human defenses.

It takes more finance to employ to an, or, ones idealists created system, than the finances used to employ the ideas to the real of the world. "Why terrorists would use the most primitive method to destroy a sky scraper building only filled in capacity of only non military trained personnel's with two hijacked airplanes. Undoubtedly, the attackers very well know that to introduce such an idea whether primitive or not, would have to create a strong defense against such an attack by the ones who have received such an attack for such as an attacker. An action has been created a reaction undoubtedly.

{2} the people who chooses the job of a politician reluctantly uses such a power to inhabit such a trait unto other foreign government by means of diplomacy but such diplomacy extends, only to the nations which such a diplomatic talks, has occur, due to this, if a citizen and noted well I might add, decide to enter into a nation that such as their government has no existing relations, then to this, such a chaos can occur if the citizen's life may be in danger by the laws existing within that nation.

Or if, there is such a relation, then how much does it extends unto the citizen traveling onto the allied nation, their true safety while visiting. To these speeches made by both existing governments are only made to benefit each other resources and their dollars unto other economies, nationwide and not the safety of foreigners or disputes, within the citizens of such a nation and the heartfelt feeling of the visitors.

Due to this existing development, the visitors or foreigners, made such a choice to enter unto another existing form of government and their existing laws, governing such as their land but their safety whilst staying unto this foreign entity, rests solely on them. Reasons to be are that, such law of the land has the job of securing all visitors and non visitors of any nation. Foolishly thinking, no nation is safe haven, is a proven underestimated statement. To all nations have their conflicts at heart whether it reveals itself unto.

To this, it must be revealed, that citizens of any nation must not rely solely on any form of government to decide upon their own safety. To this, government spend all their optimum of measures and efforts creating systems to defend themselves against any "inland invasion" at home rather than seek the interest of the foreigners visiting such a nation, until such visitors create a system to invade the existing government by corrupting the mind of the citizens, residing, in such a nation, until the citizens, uses such a system to employ, all their efforts, may it be to disrupt the functions of a government.

The idea of me ever joining a uniform organization has crossed my mind but which system shall my intelligence be bestowed unto, these government trained soldiers.

If I join and represent any such system, I must remain rational in all Endeavors to such feats, which I am a soldier in a uniform and not the uniform, that defines that I am a soldier, where I must never fight ones battle and battles of another or fight for you and your comrade, to such comrade shares a different opinion "then, why did such comrade join such a system?". Let such comrade show greatness during the shared feats or battles, then such help shall be offered to them. For I shall remain domained, if such superior beings possess more power than me. If little possession is given to me, then every opportunity must be put to the greatest test. For I need no great battlefields to win a battle but a great skill to win such battle is important. Neither do I need lots of soldiers to win a battle, for every man shall be skillfully trained in the art of defense and survival tactics, for great battles they may not posses but when the opportunity arrives surely they can prove a great point.

And this is what I hope to achieve and because of this I will give to you a:

Personal credo on battlery skills: Possession may be less or battles may be little But when it's within my grasps, I'll strike Hard and to this "legends" are created when the End is near and nothing is accomplished from Me and my combattor and an opportunity Strikes that gives me a grasps due to their faith Or the sudden improvement of our behaviour Shall give me a winning stride to victory and is Only a victory if I the soldier pushes hard with a Determined mind and a body to follow.

To when these two powers individually increases, it becomes superpowerful: welcome yet again to a new aspiration on two of mans inner strengths. Mans traits, mans accomplishments.

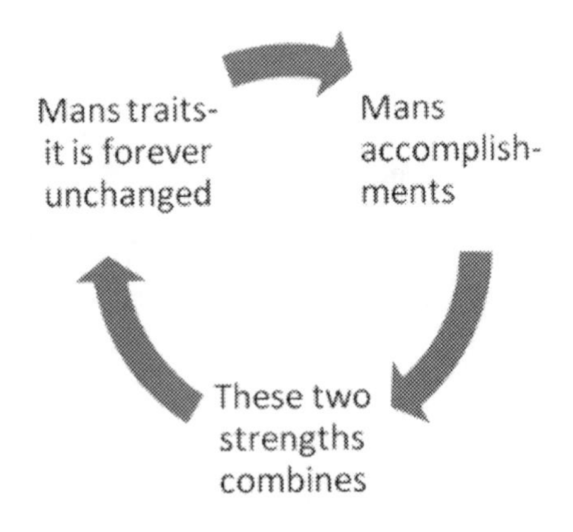

The birth of a child, is of great significance to both adult parent, or bringer of the child and to the world, for the child intelligence to be used to fill vacancies of mans interventions for their upgrowth in inventive minds. For selfish gains of the controller. But to some child their intelligence becomes noticeable and to this their traits are being developed at a tender age, thus increasing their "accomplishments"

60yrs-participation of gaining knowledge from "governing" unto people for "man
Or to God—until death"

30yrs-
& {Period of fixation on 1 agenda}
20yrs-
10yrs-participation of what's the government has to offer of education purposes
5yrs-accomplishments of feeling of strangeness, sees the un ordinary.

The period of fixation, deals with the child ability to be sucked unto mans own purpose to use your intelligenated mind for "destruction" or to be an "idealist dictator". The only way, this type of behavioural pattern can be shown are for traits of government or governance on people. But to some reasoning, these powers can only come from within the child bearer and not forgetting higher powers. The power starts to behold unto different "hands", different "actions", different "results"—until death.

You have observed and have given access to this box of intellect. Penetrated You have. Take note: that your brain can develop into a objective scenery of Thinking only if you know how deep the brain can be entered. When you see a Situation, never think around this situation, for this is how many human beings Think and their solutions are few because they see what the eyes can picture a scene without even testing the brain for other possible theories but when you Think into a situation like eyeing down a box and the only way to penetrate it Is by a staring competition and by doing this practice the mind becomes focused On one idea trying to enter this box of no entry. Yes you will begin to try smashing it or beating it out but this is physical action but with the mind is More than two actions you can carry this box to a laboratory and experiment it

This experiment can go many ways to open its presence. This is tiresome but when you treat the mind like this, you then become an "idealist" a creator of all odds. If you add a fanatics of uniform to this caliber you are then called a "uniform idealist".

Listen here now my "atorian" this is just a few of my intellect on this art. Understand this art form well and study how to think and use your brain because the less you do everyday the more others will and when war fare arise your

"DEAD MEAT"—YOU HEAR!!!!!!!!!!.

TO CONQUER THE MIND-THEIR DISEASE NOT TO USE IT—TO DESTROY IT—TO WAGE WAR TO IT.

CHAPTER XI

The art to survive.

SCROLL{1}

OH!!!!!!!!!!! How I have mastered this and I will crucify.

Solderism is no joke-the art to study how to defend, how to become discipline and not scream like a wuss when hardship arises. The body can get into a lot of stress the body will then learn to adapt.

Understand this and understand this well, this ator, is no joke, survival is what makes: the strong to stay alive and weak to die:

Yet again the line is for to sign_________________________________ ______.

Are you ready!!! Are you ready!!! Are you ready!!!

Commandments of battleries

The success of battleries—to win all rivalries-to approach the final "war"

{1} one must posses the skills of misconception and strength from the usage of the hands to the cunningness of the brain "the will of misconception"

{2}one must possess the knowledge of governance-to governance are the properties of battleries. The source of its duration. The will of controlling properties.

{3}one must possess the true active motions of not honouring the decisive code of distributing "humans errors" in every battle

{4}one must possess the measures of being undefeated occasionally to not lead it to the extrodinare

{5}one must possess the counterability to not take side, whether good or evil. To make decision upon greatness which comes upon performance and not possessing good will.

{6}one must possess the knowledge of the "scriptures to greatness" that comes from battles and to remember to achieve to betterment of war. An ator must win all battles. For each battles has their own name. For their names must be relinquished. The will of educating the spirit of defeating all battles without a loss.

{7}one must possess the understanding of life and no other of this world is considered an ators right hand in battles. The will to always conjure plans of deceit

{8}one must possess all understanding of all battles that comes with the commandments. Tyrannies of the Me5

{9}one must possess the psyche of human emotions, dwealth with understanding of success. To lengthily give it forms of illusion. To that of controllable by the ator.

{10}one must possess the skills to put all "thoughts to sleep"—to sleep to thought.

The will to put dreams to real

{11}one must possess boldness, courage, skills for these are words showing these simple outwards, make great contributions to their destruction

{12}one must possess the chaotic mind in possession in the world. To show their chaotic-cy, which is part of the ators emblem.

{13}when there are too many different types of forces, there are always inaccuracies in judgement, overcoming the overwhelming strength. For this the commandment of battlery states: to many forces are shown but shows no comparities for success. These forces must be located and destroyed and so being their strength would be noted.

{14}if a combatant posses the will to fight, ask the fighter the purpose to fight. Then declare a "battle of respect" on the combatant and any defiant. To let their tongues be silent, when the ator punishes them for being a combattor, other than a human emotioner.

{15}one must possess the important skill of "theology" and to always know the territories before battlery begins. "the will of defining methods of successful winnings."

{16}systems matures—revolves—mutates to the ator that seeks controlment of system must be noted—systems mutates unnoticingly, in effect it is right to condone actions of this new system, whereas fails-system of the "old regimic" must take effect to destroy shields of emblem to further pursue course of action of anti action development to control the new system. This means the new system becomes an old system. When the ator defeats it. But life on earth is competitiveness for survival. The world evolves where the old regimic system must remain for further development in case a mutated strain of a system is evolving.

For this is a golden rule of obtaining battlery. The will to understand that system mutates—to controlling must be the both old and anti controlment regime and must be placed together to destroy the mutated system-the circles revolves.

-System mutates means-

1st-system shows similar attributes as shown of the latter controlment before it mutates but its strength is more powerful and advantages are shown-by upgraded weaponrycounter attacks.

2nd-new system has evolved showing no comparison of any old system ever in existence and its strength is more powerful than its source. To conquer this new system comes by a lot of "challenges"—mastering this system may be futile.

3rd-system that is mobile-this system goes whenever it pleases. Picking resourceful sources to its trial. But these trails of sources do not last long towards counter attacking. But to find this system to control is very much impossible due to its inpenetratable shield to fight every system attacks whenever it crosses territories. It's not a destructive system, it's will is to understand all forces of systems in evolution.

4th-this system is the system towards "governance" and its existence has been since the evolution of mankind. This system is frequently used by man, seeking great power. Turning these people into their own domain. This system feeds on mans intelligence to keep it surviving to only conquer and rule, now called:

Mans system of interventions

A]. for man also feeds on this system for their own survival

B]. for this is what makes the world evolves.

17th-it is a must that to some individuals, their best is not always their best until they meet someone who is better than their best or madness creates the atmosphere. To that of an ator, the gift of seeing this is a optimum. Which is looked as a favourable opportunity for a battle, which would be greatly loved.

18th-it is a must when asked by a challenger that the ator must accept. To the ator must upgrade the skills needed in all forms of battlery

Once a challenger, twice a competitor, 3 times a match, 4times a deathmatch.

19th-never belong to an organization where different bodies exists where obscured goals exists. Betrayal would be imminent. It is a must to all soldiers fighting under the ators command must be subjected to the destruction of their own lives. Where times of witnessing are prevalent.

20th-the most important "element" of the body is the "human mind". The most important "life" of the body is the "heart". Without the both, substainity would not prevail, the bodies fail.

Forms of destruction of the human being

{Am1}.human mind—dormant, alone, accessing the vulnerability, for upgrowth Remains particularly contracending

{Am2} heart-the heart reeks havoc, pain, disturbance of the highest. To the Cursed one, the heart is no longer an important element but a tool of Strength in times of conundrums

{Am3} hunger-simultaneously, efforting, the belly of the beast. The source of its Strength lies onwards.

21st-one must possess the knowledge and to always keep in thought that the systems created by mans intelligence cannot be named as a successors-due to the systems collapse unique at times of troubles. For this is the method of battlery comes to the system. For battlery done unto the unchallengers. May their God rest them in their dyer need.

22nd-it is a dyer must, to all soldiers must seat their bow to accomplish any feats desired by the ators heart. To do other would be death by distributions. The will to use the strength to accomplish any feats ahead.

23rd-the ator must know perceivingly that the position of life and to the beliefs of ownership of lifeis singularly in the hands of the beholders. The beholders of life and to take it away.pays a heavy price at the end.

24th-it is a must to the ator that if you massacre, then the toleration of the ator living in succession would be to a minimum lifespan:

{Am1} to the rule of battlery states: the destruction of many beings are the Destruction of your own

{Am2} if acts are not prohibited then destroying defiants till their lifespan is no more to encounter, then so shall it be done to you at the coming of the ators end

{Am3}to the rule states-the ator must never flee for their own destruction. For then the generated systems to come to the present future would be more devastated than predicted. Generations brings forth new breeds of strength to destroy good, evil, bad or subtly ators of the world

25th-one must perform the act of controlment of battlery. The act of commanding large segments of "intrusions-in-high-capabilities". I.W.H.C. is a continuous succession.

26th-the art to be deadly in ways of intelligent schemes to the way of the tongue. The ator must realize that contented emotions are not prohibited for no human are your "combattors at arms"

NB—for all must be destroy to conquer—for self must come to point out Destructive emotions triggered by endless competitions made by any Atorians—for the human race must see you as a conqueror and you must be Hated.

27th-for the true best of the ator-the ators best comes from their usage of intelligence against odds of mutated forces at arms. The art of silences, the art of comouflagement. For the ator must not seek a singular objective, for many tasks are ahead. Mobility are the test of resilience, until time are great.

28th-remember to plan for tasks ahead, to never leave unwanting emotions of beings failures. For failures are never an option—it's a curse.

29th-to every battles-the ator seeks success To the battler or the atorians must remember to never do battles with half your skills or half plan of action. To win battles comes wittyness, skills, strengths, madness. For these combines, comes powerful attempts for certainty.

30th-the atorians must never be blunt to situations when being approached. For the rule of power is to never accept liars or cheaters as your own. For they must be destroyed.

31st-the ator must command the single obstacle plaguing the human race of their inefficiency. The art of efforting and to its singular purpose. For mankind can make themselves be a creator or destructor of all things possible.

32nd-the ator at the beginning of every battle must reveal himself and the purpose behind the conflicted interest at bay. To remind the combattor that the ator is privileged to have met in this special occasion where battles stands at the only option for survival.

33rd-the ator must remember every commandment goes with the emblem head and to that head of battlery is served by the importance of life.

34th-the ator must let the combattor strike first. In this p-o-action. The ator can asset any disparities in the form the combattor takes to destroy the ator and to use it to the advantage by the ator.

{1}non responsive action—where the ator strikes last, beholding the ator to use all the resource at their disposal. In taking and analyzing the combattor form of action

{2}in forceful entry action-where the ator goes into the mind of the combattor by using the art of trickery and manipulation. Deceiving the combattor with his own senses. The senses must be activated at its highest to defeat the combattor. Seeing things they want to see, seeing things they don't want to see. In any rate these two gives of an action by the combattor revealing themselves. Remember any given information, must be analyze and tested against the combattor. Where there is no remorse of action that are about to occur. Where there is one golden rule:

{an enemy is always an enemy} no debates—no truce—just annihilation.

Note well survival is a key element to understanding the flowdarity of how the elements fits well together. The ators learning don't have to follow my pattern but can teach you what commandments are and ways to include such to you work force plenty in the system.

Here is another for you: 3rd order of controlment to demise camouflage.

{1} any system such persons must be foreclosed unto, non the less, must respect its co formalities

{2} movement must be made secretly and quietly. One must seldomly know your movements.

{3} the straight and narrow paths must be attained, knowledge of your representation would be seen even when off duty. Make plans and stick to it, any diversions must be ignored.

{4} one must be careful to when talking to even those who represent you "at arms".

{5} remember, no matter representing a nation, a supreme leader of a unit will always have this to say—"anyone can do this job" even one of little judgement. Remember no matter how good you are, a leader would always look down at you and make suggestive comments that you are not the best, so as in government occupations. Competition is highly anticipated, so look out for betrayals.

{6} one must be good to those who are not fortunate, to not have opportunities. There can be simple civilians that are more powerful than those who represent their oppoutunists.

{7} one must remember, money is not all. One must train the body profusely, challenge the body and find your weakness before others can and be warned of civilians interpretations, likewise the superficial that's not there, but present itself.

{8} one must always remember the system you represent that are controlled by men who written such laws, that are not of your own and heed the support of men themselves, is represented as a ghost. To us, you represent a ghost that has no power and uses the will of men to institute them. Without men to institute them, it then becomes powerless. Destroy the man that does, then your destroying its effectiveness.

And due to this, one must be careful when enacting the law amongst civilians. Note, this ghost has no form, no shape of colour, only mans emotion and shape and colour can be represented, so are their emotions, so be noteful what can be expected.

{9} one must note the destruction of the "machines" we use as arms. As methods to win all human attributal goal, for there are no other way human can thrive together than the inventions to kill and noticing this, shall tell you how unsuperior humans are.

{10} one must not, shall not, shed no mans blood and their controlive laws Governing you to act accordingly to such, follow that of your own.

{11} one must be a patriot to such system in recongnisation of unpowerless citizens and for the weak at heart but one must acknowledge the flawless within such systems. Thus, one must speak of it, let them hear your voice, if no changes shall occur, one must leave such system to one with less danger.

Let get this straight and to the point my atorian. Regardless of what system you represent, may it be by civil service or more patriotic acts like wearing a uniform or governing the ruleship of citizens, one must love their country for at the beginning of time the founders of these systems spent most their lives and effort to create what some people take for granted. Be the one to find the errors and correct them, be the one that support change no matter what philosophy governs your action. Make an impact in this societal efforts of mankind—this, the 21st century.

In number {8} mention was made about a "ghost". A ghost is in reference to government and governance or systems as it's called. These systems has no form of power and due to this the power is only exerted from those who wields its power and creates the continuation of its power. So noted a system is a ghost, where man has given a name due to their type of creation to their type of rulement, their type of ideology behind its substance.

Commandments of solderism—shield must prevail

To describe oneself as a "survivalists" one must indeed undertake measures to accompany such great word. What you are about to witness are the wonders of solderism and its greatness amongst idealists.

{1} it must be done, that soldiers must be of the uttment and athletic built

Always.

{2} it must be done that whenever travels are concerned, always go to the directions and never sidetrack to another destination unless felt to.

{3} it must be done one must travel "alone" if accompanied do less conversating and more surveillance.

{4} it must be done that, no soldier must carry weapons, believe in your training. One must carry a disposable weapon made of disposable materials or unidentified as weapons.

{5} it must be done that, one must prevent confrontations or speaking in a aggressive manner, control speaking is the choice all the way. If given leeway one must not fight amongst crowds or individuals. Measures must be done in a discreet manner

{6} it must be done that the conversations on race\religion is forbidden and even mention. To if one do not know then advice such persons that individuals are broken down into groups then into groups then into systems then into competition of such system, to the world views are different. Systems of representations are what it is looked upon.

{7} it must be done that one must find an occupation with less stress, this improves your physical physique. You need not need a job for powerful means or force. Just one that is stress risk free and less labour of the mind and body.

{8} it must be done that, one is not forbidden from other practices other than these but note, survival techniques and ways of living must be practical and learnt to its highest conformities. And to this, then such individuals can apply such pressures towards their outwards look upon society.

Note that what was written is of the truest of all truth and note it can

Never be said no other way.

I AM NO PATRIOT TO NO LAND "NEITHER" TO NO CREATIVE SYSTEM BUT I CHANNEL MY EFFORTING FORCE TOWARDS IMPROVEMENT OF HUMAN CONTINUAL, SUPERIOR MIND, WITHIN A UNIFORM AND THEIR EXISTENCE, AMONGST ALL LANDS AND THEIR DIFFERENCES.

SCROLL{2}

Welcome atorian and all you have shown its presence unto, great are you the reader, that shows those you know, that is worthy to understand this truth of a prophesy not only the beginning arts but this as well. For without this art, their can be no discipline for the others to ever become an idea to the pigmented minds. Great are you—but not unto me, for there are a lot of hidden secrets that lies behind the ones, that for generations that have past, has earned names to their despicable works by non idealists, who today, still tries tirelessly to uncover their minds at work and how they function. Witness this, this is just a few of how us, uniform supremist warlord thinks. For our title is a laughter to our minds at work.

WARNING TO THE NON-IDEALISTS!!!!!!!!!

Let us begin the skillful art to survival: This physical aspect noted well to its conformities show you combat strategies. The pictures and quotations that were illustrated are not introduced into your format of learning, for fear of the abused and misused of this art to combat a combattors will to continue a fight. The use of advance technology, would guide you to destroy a combator. But not well, that whenever a dictator is rising to the scenes, who perhaps wears a uniform, then of course this idealist has to "create new methods of survival for their soldiers to learn", so it is with a creation of a new system.

You may not have known this but these styles, are not seen in any form of informative medium you can entertain yourself but failure will guide your efforts. Note also I am a warlord in existence and don't expect me to offer you all that I have.

Know this—the aim of combating the technique of incisions on the body must be performed, vividly, fastly, prescionally, swiftly, artly. Practice makes it perfect.

Be warned—all techniques can be used at once the consequences can be futile to reverse, once triggering. There are {11} eleven basic techniques. I introduce to you B.L.E.E.D.

Basic literacy of egotism of conquering enemies domain.

There are many basic-this only but one. Capturing the intensity of the body.

Let's begin with the head:

The head is made up with a brain, cranium. The brain is the inner part of the head, made up with all the important mechanisms of the human beings adaptability for growth and the usage of the intelligence. The only way the brain can use its intelligence is only by the exercising of it. The brain is a significant character on its own.

The cranium is the exterior part of the head. Its duty is to protect the interior of the head, called the brain base network or brain base. It's a fact that the brain is a network of beauty. The cranium can suppress little or no amounts of "blunt force" acting on it. The hardest part of the head likely to act as friction is the top of the head, unlikely the front. Notice that the cranium does not cover the opposing force action of the head. We all know that the face is an open target to brute force, so is the side of the head or side of face.

The whole of the face which reaches to the base of the temple shots is supplied with soften exterior that if pressure is applied this muscle intensifies and controls the pain inwards to the bone which is close. These muscles supports the function of the bone and nothing more, whereas there are some that have a greater function.

Applying force unto the head is a very technical attempt due to the usage of huge amounts of power, strength, effort.

1st-the aim is to not damage the fingers during the first attempt.
2nd-not to hit directly unto the "face" no matter not being protected. Its defense is that it is also a part of the "skull" just covered with "skin" helps the features of a human personality.
3rd-applying a lot of force unto the face puts the combattor unto the ground quickly and bleeding but it does not give an advantage in a fight. The combattor can easily counterattack due to facts that whenever applied effort is tried unto a big part of the body esp. the face which is the head command of senses on the body jerks an reaction, readily and attempts to hit the other combattors face. For the face is the easiest target and the only target to decrease the levels of performance even the match persists.

RULE OF FORCE: the rules are simple, basic. The three points are the temple, neck, between the eyes or forehead.

{1}hit directly unto the temple. A 2 feet distance must be attained. The closer you are the better the use of the elbow, legs and hands. The idea of martial science is used. The feet can also be used to strike at the temple shots.

The importance of this method is that no matter the effect applied unto the head, a frictional force is produced unto the "neck area". To that of the targeted area. Usage of the neck area is optional and is proven to be a area of un comfortness, for punches are.

{2} the human body is very specific to rapture but not immune to attacks. For the Importance of attacks are never to attack with the same method. For one stroke can affect the whole symphony of the body for life. Bruises, blots, concussions, traumas, uniform cuts, dislocated joints, fractures.

APPLICATION OF FORCE: THE HEART.

The heart is between the two lungs. The centre where it lies. The heart is protected with the hard caseining of the rib cage, diaphragm which extents upwards unto the tip of the chest and the muscles surrounding the chest.

{1} the attack comes from the vertical. This method is used above the chest. To initiate a full compase "kill" is to hit below the diaphragm. In this case a sharpe edged device is appropriate and the sole idea is different. The method are to use the force of the hand to stick the weapon upward using a 45 degrees angle.

Step one-chest incision

Step two-diaphragm incision

Step three-collar bone target, to a horizontal incision.

Note that there is no immediate effect onto the heart, the ultimate goal are to give damage to the surroundings area of the heart. Must apply a force unto the pressure to accomplish great results.

APPLICATION OF FORCE: THE STOMACH-DIAPHRAGM

Similar lessons are with the both targets of the destruction of the stomach and the weakening of the surround defenses of the heart. This method includes the directed hit below the diaphragm and is the only force of hit unto the stomach; other attacks will come from the "waist targets". The stomach area is vulnerable to attack, due to its non limited resources of defense would only come from the combattor.

APPLICATION OF FORCES: THE WAIST

The waist is a muscle of gratìvational movement. Without its special use. The use of moving the legs is futile. At the side of both waist one must puncture a huge wound unto them. There is also the combine force of destruction of the stomach area but my friend it remains for my soldier. The strength of the intestines lies below the waist, the muscle between the pelvis. This is an essential target to produce results.

APPLICATION OF FORCES: THE CALVES

This movement comes from one action the bellowing of the body to inact the movement unto the combattor. The use of force is applied by a sharp edged device. This attack shows difficulty, strength, positioning and vulnerable to counterattacks. This attack is the attack of the "circular art" when all movement of slitting the top of the foot uses this attack of "arcmonicle"

The application of force of all three, the top of foot, the top of ankle, the top of toes. All uses the similar application of calves. The maneuverability likewise its efficiency for upgrowth. The top of foot-a slitting movement around the ankle would penetrate a successful attack of deepening the attacker use of escaping The top of ankle-use this attack for non escaping. The top of toe-use this method frequently due to its vulnerability to a defeater Using a seated position. To arise conquerable after a gruesome attack. The Weapon surely strikes blowly unto the toes or the tendons attached unto the toes.Disabling the foot weakens the legs, destroys the presence of synapse impulse From the spine.

APPLICATION OF FORCE: HANDS

The hands are the most important force used in combating a combattor and Disabling its source of power would remain a vital product. Severing the biceps Is an elusive goal of combattors to their source of power lies in strength, effort, Energy.

{1} using a horizontal attack unto the hands is very impossible yet futile in attempts.

{2} using a vertical attack unto the biceps is very easy to plot due to its successful rate of being an easy target.

{3} using a vertical attack improves the vulnerability of the body. Front way in the attack, with or without targeting the hands only.

THE RULE OF FORCE

The rules of the force, the weapon in this attempt must be to remember that the biceps is a muscular energy trapped between the bone structure of the hands. The hands is outlined as a singular elemental structure of the body's conquerable means for gainment.

APPLICATION OF FORCE : THE WRIST

Discovering the importance of the wrists capabilities would improve the mentability of the fighter, why? it is necessary to destroy the wrists. The wrists are connectiong bones of the hands to the fingers, whilst pivoting end bones and cartilages surrounding the bones features. Simple process of annhilatement, simple process of assemblement.

Destroying the capabilities of the combatant's wrists ensures that defeat is likely, unless the combators improvise. Improvisation is a must during battles.

CONVERSATION TO NOTE:

The attacks noted in B.L.E.E.D. is but the basic. Few at numbers but are the most elusive attempts to guarantee a successful "win" against any combattors attempt to disintegrate any ator. It remains benefital to me but not to you, with failure of the in-depth aptitude to its disguises. These arts are to be performed with a sharp edged device you choose with exception of the first art, which establish the forceful attack to your opponents head.

As we end this short art of survival, you and I know that survival is a mutated system. Advancement has occurred since the beginning of the earliest battles known to us well. With these advancements, come advancements with the outfit such individuals wear entirely. However under the demise, I am aware that you have learnt nothing in this art, for I have tried entirely for you the reader, not to learn as much when comes to survival, because survival can only come from the spirit inside of you, that hence, gives you warrior fortitudes. For not all can fall victor less. Ha!!!!!!!!! Ha!!!!!!!.

CHAPTER XII

The art of uniformity

Oh!!!!!!!! The dream to see the uniform marching for their continual survival has come. For the day of their rising for I cannot tell you.

Understand this and understand it well—a uniform as mentioned is a representation of a government, for all uniforms follows the directive of a system always. Never would you see the uniform not in directives. This ensures that a stable government is in order. Unstable government never gets the appreciation of the uniform, for the uniform here is not in directive to the government, due to one reason, the policy type of rulement. One aspect one can see about the uniform, is that they will always follow uniformity and the discipline that follows it. Politicians however, never follows uniformity, for their agendas are always corrupted.

Welcome to the understanding of the uniform, creation of a uniform, creation of a uniform system. Place your signature, for I believe it will be the last signature you will have to do, because after this your hands will be so idle, your hands will be destroyed.

Ha!!!!!!!!!!!!! ha!!!!!!!!!!!!! ______________________________.

SCROLL{1}

Before this art begins, you must understand that there are always philosophies that follows every trepidations, before your time and mines as well. And knowledge of their existence is very important because ideas remain an idea only when it is not seen in the real of the world.

I am to present to you, the inner source of a government and their conformities, that follows: Welcome to the powers that may be.

The only powers a politicians has in existence is the judiciary and the police, for these powers are shadows cast out, of, from the existence of governments. The military do not exists within these politicians ideology, although ridiculously, belongs to a nation and its people choice of freedom to join such.

Can politicians destroy a "military system?" never!!!!!!!!

For the military system is a system that was derived from the inner self of a human being. The will to survive made possible by the feats we encounter. It is not a system born out of governments and philosophers but a system that was used to conquer over diplomat's way, of having conversational meetings and decision. Now these diplomats uses the military system, to show its effectiveness, which are control by human beings and yet are treated with the utmost disgrace.

The police system is grown to be more superior than the military system in democratic nations. Be very mindful, the day shall come when the military system shall become the most powerful new entity than any other system, due to its unique collaborations of "survival strength" and a "superior brain base of governance".

These two powers that fall so closely under government and their laws, are so tightly embedded that if one finds to produce its strength or losses its capacity of strength, all other elements surrounding these three powers, will also "collapse" thus adhering to a coup-e-tat.

The military comes in and fails, due to rebellious soldiers, thus, creating a new formulated system, which are control by high ranking soldiers, thus creating prolongment of a coup-e-tat, thus creating the reality of a "overthrownment", thus creating membership rulement of both the rebellious citizens and the rebellious soldiers. Thus, creating a new government under the same regimic systems but of a different style of controlment.

Note to reader: the police system, are not as supreme as the citizens, as well as the democratic leaders may think. To this it means, that if ever the destruction of the political arena or the parliament, then the judiciary takes over the leadership and instituted, that the laws created by the politicians, has been destroyed and the judiciary which has all and with the exception their own powers, exercise the laws pertaining to a nation. The judiciary will act in accordance, to rebuilding the citizen's confidence, of still remaining in the nation during their livelihood.

The military has been destroyed due to not responding to legally, about the judiciary being in supreme control. To this, it can cost chaos and it will. If the judiciary is destroyed, then the police system becomes non-existence, it can occur differently, if the "police system" is destroyed then the judiciary will need a new system to introduce all powers of the land, to, a new force and it can never be the "military" thus instituting "martial law".

The politician, judiciary, police are all systems in "one".

{M1} destroying one, one has to act

{M2} destroying all, the military acts

{M3} destroying all, the rebellious systems are introduced to rule the nations and thus creating a "new government" that may be a system in ruleship that the citizens would be infringed of their rights, to ever obtain a "vote" of balloting a new governance.

WHAT FREE THINKING UGH!!!!!!! : penetration of this knowledge is wise.

SCROLL{2}

Creating a system is indebted to the creator and you shall see how atorian.

The combative aggressors & the combative opponent

On

Many relative systems to be introduce to the real of mans

Dominion statues

Hear me now!!! To this I write about: m I I I t a r y.

{1}knowledge of all forms of laws and constituted legislative acts of the land.

{2}effecting the laws whilst giving citizens information about their exercising freedom but very limited.

{3}effecting posttraumatic actions on the offense if being resilient, to test his\her aptitude of the beings mind and to know how the persons think and to get ahead of the action about to be committed.

{4}effecting an attitude of superiority whilst giving information about offences committed in a calm way, I shall.

{5}create a "double attitude"—being angry yet calm, being bold and bad, yet informative, being superior yet gentle. The name of the game is to be superior and intelligent.

{6}create a system between you and your "opponent" or the citizens in this case and show that you are more superior in thinking, when the citizens do not show any form of superiorness to defend him\herself or posses any knowledge of their constitutional freedom.

{7}take no sides, create no friends-you must not have no friends within the system.

{8}create a dominant system around you accept no help in any way when exercising your duty. Only give help when necessary.

{9}all opinions on the ineffectiveness of the police system shall be done home based and not on the premises of governments institutions. Create a force that is impenetrable. In the mind say only small information that are yet informative and puzzling. Due to this development I have turn to another option of creating this system, that will coincide unannonymously with the existing one. I shall create a "super cop" with super intelligence.

{10}the solderism way, can work in harmony with the police force but the option In the police are to give information and receive, for my mission in the creation of a police system, is to build a central brain network. Information, against rebellious information that collects data and analyze its productivity. effecting, a different and new approach of policing, which can resemble all forms of laws written by the intelligent yesterdays at its beginning stage, until it is proven successful, then the next approach would be as mention the use of military approach: as am about to show you:

To this I will propose a military system:

This military system proposes that every person from birth must have military training from the age of five to twelve. To this, the training level differs whilst getting older after the period of twelve. An individual will have a vote and on that vote, that individual or on reaching upon age, will have a say on what choices such individual will make to contribute to the economy. That vote will become a reality at the age of independent thinking possibly twenty one.

This is the initial stage of "national service". These aspiring minds of the future of the system would also learn the laws to which they are governed by, at the age of twelve. This shall not be an everlasting one but at their learning stage. More patriotic they shall become, hypnotized and emphasized and boastfully they can pronounce, for when adulthood reaches, they can profess their utmost "loyalty" to the system and the continuation of the longevity of the principalities.

And if any societies or community fails to recognize this endeavour, separatists they would be named.

If such individual chooses to be a "civilian" after such voting, they will be transferred to another region or sector of the nation. Where the resources lies, to feed such the economy. And to those who chooses to remain in such as the "military outfit" can find different employment in the uniform sectors.

For some military officers will be called "state guardsmen" for those are the officers who would be police enforcers. For there will be, no existence of any system as recognizable before and now. For these will be replaced by "states men" "states laws".

{1} state guardsmen-which would be the new police system. Such guards will be ranked accordingly by their intelligence and superiority.

{2} national laws-which would be the new justice system. Persons presiding over these separatists citizens are pronounced by their rank, number and stature. To these laws are to cover the civilians also any disturbance in chaotic minds to create an enemy of the state. Military or civilian citizens.

{2a} in case of citizens who wears the uniform, a new type of system would be placed to address natures of the breaking of state laws by these outfits, however, if brought to the attention, that such breaking of laws, a civilian has been the victim, then such civilians reports, to the state guardsmen, will be sufficient. No civilians shall enter this court, without wearing a uniform or either no civilians cannot implicate any uniform wearer to any courts which preside only in civilians matter.

The wearers of the military uniform are the most supreme, then the lists follows. If a military personnel has been implicated in crimes against the state, no state guards men cannot institute arrests. The files that include the information must be overseen by a higher authority or a governing uniform allegiance, if truth resides then the bearer of this outfit will no longer be part of the organization and such being would be addressing two courts. The military courts and the civilian courts.

{3} public officers-this replaces politicians{the suit and tie}. Their jobs do not differ but the use of "uniform" are permitted under the military laws. For all persons that are representing authority must wear uniform.

For this military system is a system that encourages all individuals to belong in a sector or group. No one is a singular body, to if ever any individual is discovered without being part of upliftment of the economy by means of "inventitive corps ops" the "energy corps ops" "the civilian arms"—[an arms that specifically deals with beings who have not capture, the use of their intelligent brain, are put to these arms].

Then such an individual is recognized as a treat and a national enemy and shall be placed in a combatant prison cell. Every national are free in exercising any free will but unless such a being is contributing to the society, for we believe the brain ia a important aspect.

The creation of another system called the "system of invention on the intervention"—where disputes are headed to the most utmost respect. Disputes ranged from diplomatic views, religious views also the creation of a "central shield network". Where an officer debates on the use for troops to fight battles or warfare in any part of the world including in an inland threat.

Oh!!!! how great the day will be when arisen the proclamation of dirt to dust

SCROLL{2}

The prophesy of a army warlord

An army warlord is not born into one or either have been prophesied by some doctrine due to the expansion of some individuals creativity of 'dooming age". Unless a supreme power says otherwise. To take note: being a uniform lover can come at any age if the individual prophesizes such action and believe such action to become true.

Each individual who have authoritative synopsis, chooses if such profession would be towards the reward of God or the reward of favoritism of men.

[a] the army warlord, can go through all fields of ranks, or be succeeded above all subordinating commands of ranks, due to a development that exceeds any individual who are in possession of high ranks in office.

[b] ranks must not be given only to those who passes "seniority" but to those who passes the willingness and the gift that is not norm in society.

A uniform warlord

[a] must be for his\her uniform and bearance for it.

[b] must be an exemplary, to how a uniform can become and the way it must be admired.

[c] must plan ahead to any development-being a strategist and an supremist idealist.

[d] must be the most supreme leader at the helm of all dynasties.

[e] must portray a supreme dominating look to such individual already knows hate ration, is mentionable everywhere and the many dislikes can be common.

These represent some possession of such entity existing within this world but creating a uniform warlord look; can be a real aspect in today's world. But as seen throughout history, many warlords portray a certain type of behaviour not knowingly seen by many, who divulges in secrecy, to have conversations about such individuals.

They believe God's hand has reach out of the heaven skies and bestow unto them the gift of leadership, the gift to be supreme over the subjects of the world but however, it may be true, my prophesy presence of a uniform warlord is quite different, for which I shall not divulge. The decision rests solely on the possessive individual and their motive to lead. Their reasons why are always hidden as do many leaders.

Those who posse's infinite power, makes journals of their power and ways to portray them in the subjective world of works. So as such, I can prophesize that there will always be uniform lovers, who are more lovers to themselves or either the companions of others, would always rule the workforce plenty, of a system or many of a system.

Now atorian you have been witnessed to knowledge of this uniform warlord. I have leave the best for last, where I have captured and tamed all the arts mentioned before and have provide the best of four{4} for you to rekindle on.

Let us begin with the art to conquer
The psychological warfare of the mind.

The mind of a normal individual can produce a certain degree of lengthways that are emitted through any machines, that determine mind waves and the percentage, of cell mitochondria energywhich, is produced to create an idea or ideas. This wavelength of a normal thinking everyday strategic of a person but if ever been introduced by another idea to say "an idea that interferes with such individuals normal wavelengths, a miscoursed length of waves can be seen.

Such an individual begins to strategize about such induced ideas and a creation of new ideas by themselves, such a way to combat or control the introduced idea. How a person behaves are signs on how much wavelengths is used to either control or combat it. The instant of enactment to the instant of re enactment.

Psychological warfare—is the taunting of the mind, whoever posses this quality of a gift whether learnt or introduced as a gift can become most powerful in their endeavours. But firstly one must understand the human behaviour of the beings that resides in so many fields of intelligence and how challenging it will be to control an individual feats.

Perceive ion—means doing something to come in an individual favour. If a situation arises where test of intelligence is considered, one individual may decide to take lead by one of his\her many talents and present it to the masters of the challenge.

This challenge then used in its mightiest way may or would perceive attention unto the masters. Thus forcing the other challenger to do the same in similarity to the other challenger. This causes a situation to be in your favour, one of your talents when works best produce great rewards, courage to use it is inevitable. Sometimes the masters may not be aware of this new talent and may give way to its inception.

The art of intellectuality
System Foleys

When gun manufacturers build guns for warfare their only liking comes when it goes to the hand of those that needs it in reward for billions of dollars and sponsorship. If non is provided the manufactures ends up with a lot of "steel". Their only option then is to find alternative means to receive what is owed by them.

Territorial warfare profits a lot of "hands", especially the wet ones but "how often do they come?". Drugs one of the leading manufacturing industry in the world that targets inward a system, be in turmoil or not, it finds a way in to such. If the weapons on their display can profit both business.

Here you can see how invasion to a system can arise in many forms in a system workforce.

Societal warfare can be very profitable you just have to find individuals who posses no absolute enjoyment of the system operations and individuals who can introduce it to a system without interferences. "Here is how crime is big business?" and to such society displays their forceful power into others, while the elements that reacts to such development finds it difficult to comprehend strategies.

"What price do they pay for selfdom monetary gain?" a system can easily be destroyed but difficult to rise again and if such systems is destroyed the same manufacturers who has supply for little or nothing then has the ability to supply for a lot more money by forces who have intentions to bring back democracy. "And who do you think those new inventitive weapons are for"?—to experiment the inefficiency of the weapons on you the "separatists group".

The art of survility
Mercy pledges for the combattors

Mercy is not for feigners or for the weakers, "beg please, beg please, have mercy on me". Can be a breathless approach for your unwillingness to accept the dangerous feigners, the act of total revengers. Consolidators of mercy, understand mercy, can be granted for those who beg hard and wail tirelessly for it, to be placed in your hands.

Beg hard and more hard, the uniform will pledge your dominance of mercy. Beg your allegiance for chaos, your ingenuity at work, bring chaos to the dominions. "What about the innocent mercies?" Did they beg for it as you do so unpronounced, so unnoticed, so rapid to react the proact, had no chance for mercy pledge. What about your armies of men, vibrant, so strong, so fast, so evolved, march miles in weather, to flag those begetters. For an ideal, created by a megalomania, stricken the world of phobias of fear, of being captured. Be put in those sweat box, the size of a rabbits endowment, to be exercised for information to beg for mercy the dg you are. What's plan in your head, may not of any you be off. Drill and drill, beg mercy until your blood spill out on the floor on boots on tools used to extract the roots of all problems.

Overused by generals, unused buy their finite brains, you can hear them complain in the war rooms of all rooms. If it's the bathroom, no problem to blame, their mercy too frail, begs to abstain, refrain from pain. Power over pain, tell that to the captured soldiers, who endure pain, to keep the system intact. "What tact the enemies expect to pack?" Human being can become experimental figures in the today world of information, while the mercy pledge shall remain the frightening experimatic. Re enactment to society inception of the destruction to a stable powerhouse.

Innocent mercies—are mercies of innocent individuals who are or where caught between any warring faction group. As to such individuals, represents any power of allegiances to either only to themselves. If died, such mercies are called "fallen mercies" for such individuals are not able to tell about their events so their mercy never left their tongues, falling on deaf ears.

An innocent mercy is individuals who live to tell their story which in turn is then called a "mercy pledge" of an innocent individual, To most innocent mercies told by individual more or less represent a higher power which is "God". And to this one must be careful when attempting or prophesizing warlike behaviour.

Mercy-is a powerful word which holds divine power within all human beings.

The art of uniformity

separatisms

Sepratists-are individuals who practice division within a system by any means with the use of the free exercising of rights and their freedom to act willingly, therefore the overabused of their freedom of rights given by the system, using this creative idea.

Sepratisms-is a society, group or community that wants no conformity to the likes of a system. 85% of sepratisms are introduced by creating new ways to prevent them to be close to the likes of the system. For example, creating new religions into a system, so they can bamboozled the populists and thus go so far by introducing it in the authoritative entities, to gain friendship due to in times of trouble.

They believe, these authoritative figures can rally around them. Blinding these figures by lies and vituperative animosities. But if you ask them, "what contributions they have made to the society?"-they can never answer you.

For I the atorian say and take note: for I have and would forever dislike to my bones "sepratist entities, sepratists individuals and worse civilians, who have captured the spirit in this new trend to destabilize governments. For I would say if you represent the system in any way, then do it to your best : be patriotic to your country and not patriotic to some foreigners ideas. Because here is where most separatism begins, with foreign interventionist.

I dislike terrorist and all those people who wears no uniform just some type of material that represents no disciplines and prophesizing warlike behaviours. Leave this behaviour for the "uniform outfit"

For I will leave you some end notes:

It shall never be justifiable for me the true "ator d combattor" when scripting documents to be portray in the existing system to not copy or translate any scripted words before such writings has occurred or even if such words are not written yet but is being processed in the intelligent mind undecided to be written, it shall be in presence in its own "format" and in relation to any evidence at such time. Any interference within existing words shall only be an reintroduction, towards an already happening existence but such reintroduction shall take no more than two {2} ideal, to cover an action in existence.

Note to world:

To any persons using such words written by me the true ator, without any privy knowledge of it and if being found using such words on behalf of the first ator in existence, the atorian would have no other choice to combat with such person with any objective schemes found necessary to be dealt with.

For such words shall only be "spelt" among man by the atorian, himself, or a being "chosen" by the ator to forfeit unto mans expense. But even if such beings are to be chosen, such beings must undertake a "pledge of secrecy" and undergo years of preparatory knowledgeable schematics of how the mind can think more than one way" not subjectively but prophesizing objectively".

What a trip would you say in the mind of a supreme, power, mighty, uniform warlord? Now, you are equipped to begin thinking differently than your inception mind had in the first place.

Remember this, ator, knowledge is plentiful, if you are able to read and understand this trait fully, then you intelligence have grown and is up to you to ensure it reach to the point of "pit of elimination" the dark part of the brain. Where you will be a superior mind living in the finite masses of the untamed.

Secret I am going to show you—objective thinking opens the mind and "foresight" is then a gift you have not inherited but learnt. You will then begin to witness and understand human behaviours. And prophesizing soon begets unto you.

I leave you here and now—just because you have read this book, do not mean you are equipped to handle the minds of the world or yet again me ha!!!!!!!ha!!!!!!!

For no system shall tell this superior I, how to use I power, my great power, for I shall choose how to use, where to use and whom to use it onto.

-This is my declaration of my use to my great superior power-

Your perceptive mind here has to make a decision if it presents itself in good order to be recognized as great words put together to form an intelligent point that bases itself to a great point of certainty and truth, "life" the meaning to this book and the strange humaning traits that follows it.

My art is deadly, my skill is renounced, my aim is regimental, my intelligence would become legend

"You will never discover in your lifetime a greater knowledge than this"

Sylvan lightbourne
#33 Hector street, la romaine
San Fernando
Trinidad and Tobago
Contact number-1868717-3353 miimt@hotmail.com